TRUTH OR TRADITION

Terry Johns

Copyright © 2009 by Terry Johns

Truth Or Tradition
by Terry Johns

Printed in the United States of America

ISBN 978-1-60791-270-5

All rights reserved solely by the author. The author guarantees all contents are original and do not infringe upon the legal rights of any other person or work. No part of this book may be reproduced in any form without the permission of the author. The views expressed in this book are not necessarily those of the publisher.

Unless otherwise indicated, Bible quotations are taken from The New King James Version of the Bible. Copyright © 1988 by Thomas Nelson, Inc.

GO Ministries Canada
Box 1213
Red Deer. AB.
Canada. T4N 6S6
Email: terryjohns@shaw.ca
Website: www.freechristianbook.ca

www.xulonpress.com

TABLE OF CONTENTS

Chapter 1	Thinking, Perception & Asking Questions	13
Chapter 2	Why Are We Building These Towers	25
Chapter 3	The Kingdom Of Darkness	35
Chapter 4	The Church In Babylon	43
Chapter 5	The Kingdom Of Light	59
Chapter 6	The House-Church / Cell-Group Movement	65
Chapter 7	How Did We Arrive Here?	73
Chapter 8	The Church Of The Kingdom	95
Chapter 9	Church Defined By Love Not Structure	103
Chapter 10	Numerical Growth	117
Chapter 11	Escaping Through the Fire	121
Chapter 12	The End And The Beginning	127

GO MINISTRIES CANADA was pioneered by Terry & Christine Johns. Based in Red Deer, Alberta, Canada, we are a non-profit association of people who believe we are living in the last days and that Jesus is calling His Church back to Biblical foundations. *1 Cor 12:28 And God has appointed these in the church: first apostles, second prophets, third teachers, after that miracles, then gifts of healings................*

For more information on **GO MINISTRIES** and a list of other publications written by us, please contact us via the details above.

ACKNOWLEDGEMENTS

I wish to acknowledge the input I have received over these years from my peers and those to whom I have looked for guidance and teaching. I wish to pass on a special thanks to my darling wife Christine, Roy Baylis, Les & Jean Turner, Robin & Pirrko Johnson and Paul & Liz Halfter, who have faithfully read and re-read the draft copies of this book, without their wisdom and input it would still be unfinished. I am deeply grateful to my family who have tolerated, supported and loved me as I have struggled through the implications of the things I have been learning. Often they have suffered rejection by those they thought to be friends as a result of my relentless pursuit of truth. Most of all I am thankful to the Lord for His patience with me. I have been slow to learn, and have often been wrong, but He has never given up on me, and even to this day continues to teach me new things. Truly He is faithful to His promise to be with us always!

I dedicate this book to the millions of Christians across the globe whose uncompromising pursuit for truth above tradition is perceived as a threat by denominational Christianity. May this book be an inspiration to you all.

AIMS AND OBJECTIVES

In this book we will be looking mostly at the institutional church - the relationship that believers have with it and its compatibility with the Kingdom of God as revealed in the Scriptures. We will be asking if, over the past 1700 years, the traditions of men have gradually usurped the authority of the Bible. We will seek to understand why discussions about the problems that exist within institutional Christendom generate such passion, fear and hostility. We will look at why people seem so motivated and anxious to defend the system. Is this similar to the passion that Jesus demonstrated for His Father's Temple when He cast out the money changers? Or is it because people have invested so much of their lives and security in these structures? We will take an in-depth look at what church is.

We will ask what aspects of church are unchangeable, what are eternal and what are culturally defined? At what point do structures and practices cease to be helpful and instead become destructive? We will try to identify some of Satan's tactics for deceiving believers, and ask if indeed much of what passes as Christianity is in fact a subtle counterfeit engineered by the Prince of Lies.

These are complex questions that cannot be answered by one-line statements. Unfortunately, the nature of a book is that we can discuss only one issue at a time, which may require us to make assumptions about something that is discussed in more depth later on. Many of the comments that I have received, have been that some statements appear to be unsupported by facts. In most of these cases the supporting evidence has in fact been presented later on in the book. It is my suggestion that you read this book twice - once, fairly quickly, to get an overview of the major themes, and then again in more detail to understand the picture that the book seeks to paint. This book is not intended to be a theological treatise in which we laboriously cross every "t" and dot every "i", but rather to prompt you, like the Bereans (Acts 17:11), to examine the Scriptures even more thoroughly for yourself to see if what we say is indeed true.

Chapter 1

THINKING, PERCEPTION, & ASKING QUESTIONS

There are probably few, if any, Christians who have not, at some time, felt discouraged, helpless and disillusioned. Many of us have wrestled long and hard over the implications of seeing the Lord's Church become a radical force on the earth. Jesus said that when He returns it will be to a Church that is "radiant and without stain or wrinkle" (Eph 5:27) But what will it take for this to become a reality in our lives? What will it take for the gospel to be seen as a vital and effective alternative to the emptiness of secularism?

During the past 40 years the Church has experienced the healing revivals of the 50s, the Jesus People of the 60's and the emergence of the charismatic movement in the early 70's. This then gave birth to the restoration house-church movement of the late 70's and early 80's. All of these have stemmed from the earnest and sincere desires of believers who wanted to reach their generation with the gospel of Jesus Christ. Yet now, at the turn of the century, we are seeing a massive disillusionment with the institutional church. Statistics show that over a thousand people are leaving the Anglican Church each week! According to a BBC survey (Everyman on BBC

1, Sunday, 30th Nov, 1997), the fastest growing religion in Britain today is Paganism! Clearly there is a thirst for spirituality, but why do people not turn to Jesus? There cannot be a problem with Jesus, so could it be the "church" that is the problem? Perhaps, like us, you have studied countless books on evangelism, church planting, church growth, and cell groups in search of answers to questions such as these. Perhaps like us, you have been involved in various different ministries and styles of churches, and yet are left with the nagging conviction that none of these really gets to the bottom of the real issues. What will it take to find genuine answers to these very real questions? Certainly it cannot be easy; otherwise all the problems would have been ironed out years ago. But also it cannot be difficult, since Christ came to offer His solutions to all who would seek them, for He says "ask and you shall receive, seek and you shall find, knock, and the door shall be opened to you." The reality is that there are a number of hurdles that need to be overcome before answers can be found.

(i) Thinking Patterns
(ii) Cultural Assumptions
(iii) Resistance to Change

Thinking Patterns
The first of these is the way in which we actually think about the problem.

Linear and Lateral Thinking
When facing a problem there are two types of thinking strategy that can be used to find the solutions. The first is called linear or logical thinking. This type of thinking starts with where we are, and moves us one step at a time, with each step being a logical progression from the previous position. Linear thinking starts with "let's gather all the facts and

see where that leads us". The advantage of linear thinking is that it is very surefooted. At every step you can check back and make sure that you have not made any mistakes. The drawback is that it all depends on the initial assumptions being correct.

Suppose, for example, that you are a pirate, and have come to dig up your buried treasure on a deserted island. You have the treasure map, and you have marked the spot. So you start to dig. But after digging a while you still have not hit treasure. What do you do? There are basically two options -continue to dig to see if perhaps the treasure is buried a little deeper, or stop digging and find a different spot in which to dig.

Linear thinking is like the first option. The assumption is that this is the correct spot, therefore the treasure must be down here somewhere, and we must keep digging.

But the lateral thinker takes a different approach. He steps out of the hole, looks around and says "I wonder if we are in the right spot? Come to that, are we sure that we are on the right island?" The lateral thinker is not afraid to question the very foundations on which his actions have been based.

Most people are linear thinkers. Most "experts" are linear thinkers. When something is not working properly most people, especially most experts, will continue to use linear thinking to try to fix it. In many cases that is adequate. But to find solutions to the more difficult challenges, both linear and lateral thinking need to be employed.

This is the case with the church. For centuries people have been struggling with the problems in the church. But in trying to solve them, they have continued to dig deeper in the same hole! The worst offenders are of course the "experts" - the pastors and vicars, priests and bishops, the religious leaders. Having risen through the ranks of the institutional church their thinking has been so molded that they cannot conceive of any different way of doing things. These are like the pirates who cover the island with bore holes, unable or unwilling to consider that perhaps they are digging on the wrong island.

Unless we are willing to ask the right questions we can never find the right answers. So what is it that stops people from asking the right questions?

Cultural Assumptions

Every day of our lives we are faced with countless decisions that we have to make some trivial, such as what colour socks to wear, and some life and death, such as whether to stop or drive through a red traffic light. We give little thought to most of these decisions. Many of them are almost automatic. The reason that we are able to do this is that we have a whole set of underlying assumptions that provide a foundation on which to base all our actions. For example, we know that we must stop at a red traffic light, because not to do so is not just illegal, but is also dangerous and may result in the death of ourselves or someone else. We also know that the reason it is illegal is because it is dangerous, and we agree that doing dangerous things is bad and that having laws to make the roads safer is good. The reason that doing dangerous things is bad is because hurting humans is bad, and the reason for that is that humans are important and have worth. We do not feel so bad about killing germs, because they are of less worth than humans. Finally we know that if we drive a car into another person there will be a collision, cars are solid, as are people, and the one cannot magically pass through the other without harm, as can the ghosts we watch in the movies.

Without these assumptions as a foundation, life would grind to a halt. At every traffic light we would have to have a long philosophical discussion with ourselves as to whether or not it would be a good or bad idea to run down the pedestrian at the crossing. We would also have to think hard as to whether we should pay the shopkeeper for his goods, or just punch him on the nose, whether we should show up to work in business clothes or a swim suit, and so on. At this point you may be saying *"Well it's obvious isn't it?"* Yes it is obvious, but only because our behavior and attitudes to these questions have already been settled by the underlying assumptions that we have in place. It is important to add here that these assumptions are rarely thought through, but are a reflex created by the culture in which we have grown up and been educated.

Without cultural assumptions and norms society would collapse. But the strength and permanence of these assumptions varies, some being at a deeper, more foundational, level than others.

What we prefer.

This is the most superficial level, and therefore the one in which there is the most variation and the most freedom to disagree or not conform. Fashions operate at this level. A few decades ago it was assumed that every working man would wear a suit every day of his life. To not conform was permissible, but would certainly cause comment or raised eyebrows. Today the fashion has changed and will, no doubt, change again. Much of this is simply preference, with no value judgment, but some of these changes represent a shift in underlying beliefs and attitudes, e.g. in attitudes to work, marriage, sex, spirituality, and respect for authority, etc.

What is good or bad?

This is the level of value judgments. Society as a whole will have a high level of agreement about what is good or bad, and these values will underlie our preferences. Being clean is, in British culture today, seen as a Good Thing. As a result, our preferences have to do with what type of soap or vacuum cleaner we like, rather than whether we need any soap at all. This was not the case just 200 years ago when people used to bath just once a year, and would throw their rubbish, and the contents of their chamber pots, out of the window onto the streets below. The streets stank of sewage, and the people smelt of sweat. No one complained of this at that time, so how did it change?

What is true or false?

In the 18th Century germs did not exist (or at least that was the cultural assumption). At that time diseases were known to be caused by bad blood, demons, and witchcraft. Since the perception was that there were no germs there was no reason to try to be clean. Instead, to cure disease one had to let out the bad blood, either by leeches or by cutting, and or to get the priest to exorcise the evil.

Big change was about to take place.

All that changed when germs were discovered in just the 19th Century by Louis Pasteur; and as a result, hospitals were cleaned up, milk was pasteurized, and people started to wash themselves. New information changed the whole set of assumptions on which society was operating. But such change did not come easily. Indeed the whole notion that something so small as to be invisible was the cause of disease was laughed at being so preposterous as to be unthinkable by any sensible human being.

In the 1400's everyone knew that the Earth was flat, and that the sun went around the Earth. No sensible thinking man would even dream to question this. When Columbus set out in 1492, for gold, glory and God, he was very literally risking his life on his conviction that it was round, and that he could open up a new trade route to India by traveling west instead of east.

What is real?

In the 19th Century, western society knew that God created Heaven and Earth, Mankind was made in God's image, and that when people died they went either to Heaven or Hell. All of society was built on this foundation and structured by traditions developed by the Church over the centuries. British justice, which forms the basis for the judicial systems of all English speaking countries, was founded on the Biblical instruction to believe the best of people (1 Cor 13), and to only convict when a crime has been proven by more than one witness.

All of this solid foundation of what was deemed to be real and true, was thrown into turmoil by the new scientific discoveries. The seeds had certainly been planted in previous centuries, but it was in the Victorian age that all these assumptions were challenged, for example by the discovery of germs and the publication of Darwin's *On the Origin of the Species*. One cannot begin to explain the flat spin that these new discoveries had on modern man of the day. All gave rise to new questions. All the assumptions of the age were turned upside down. Today, the foundations of society are shifting again. Now everyone knows that disease is caused by germs, radiation, pollution, unhealthy lifestyles, etc, and therefore our behavior has changed as a result; it has become the norm.

Are these assumptions, on which today's society is based, really true?

The Flat Earthers "knew" that their assumptions were true. Now we laugh at them. The 17th century doctors and priests "knew" that their assumptions were true. Now we see them as hopelessly primitive. How will the assumptions of today look to the citizens of the next century?

The Church is, of course, not immune from all these influences. Many assumptions have been built up over the centuries. In each era, like the assumptions in society, they have been accepted as the norm unchangeable and un-challengeable. But with passing time they have been challenged, and have changed. The great Protestant Reformation is the most obvious example. Yet, even in the centuries following, there have been more and more challenges, and changes, to the assumptions of the church. It would be arrogant for us to assume that the process has finished, and that what we now understand as Church is the final, definitive, and totally Biblical Truth.

Resistance to Change

But there is more than just our linear thinking and cultural assumptions that hinder people from asking questions and challenging assumptions. Most people have invested their lives into the church as they know it. In it, they have found security and a sense of belonging. To it, they have given their time and their money. When they have had questions or doubts about it they have been reminded that none of us are perfect, and have been warned not to fall out of fellowship with other believers lest they become backslidden. The leaders have invested even more. Their whole lives, finances, housing, social network, and purpose in life have been centered on the church, as they have known it.

To question all of this provokes much fear and anxiety. "Have I been wrong all these years? Have I given my life to something that is just a work of flesh? Have I really missed the best of God and settled for mediocrity and security? How am I supposed to live, if all that to which I have given myself is but 'hay and stubble'? "

In finding answers we will also find that we have to combat a lot of internal resistance to the change that the answers demand of us. A survey conducted in the early 90's by the (British) Daily Telegraph demonstrated a dramatic difference between North Americans and Britons in how change is perceived. To the Brits, change is a necessary evil that is met with reluctance, resistance and fear. For the Americans, change is an exciting opportunity, a chance to try something new, a chance to improve on the old. The difference is probably rooted in the fact that the New World was opened up and populated by adventurous pioneers who were dissatisfied with the status quo of the Old World. But it is this difference which has, perhaps, been one of the biggest determinants of the America's phenomenal economic and political prominence.

In Romans 12:2 Paul says, *"Do not be conformed to this world, but be transformed by the renewing of your mind, that you may prove what is that good and acceptable and perfect will of God."* We cannot expect to experience the fullness of what God has for us unless we are first willing to change. The change that is required of us is not just a superficial mental assent. It is a total restructuring of our lives, our beliefs, our convictions, our lifestyles, our finances, the way that we relate to people, the way we think, and the way that we perceive and understand the world about us. All of this has to be brought into line with the way that God sees things, rather than the way that the world does. If we are to interpret accurately the things that are happening around us, it will demand of us a totally new way of looking, seeing, and understanding, and will alter even the questions that we ask.

As Christians, we are called into a life of change. But we need also to be aware of the other factors that motivate us all to accept or resist change. The early 90's Daily Telegraph article on "Perceptions of Change" clearly highlights the issues that arise when change is encountered. As God's people we are called to be ambassadors of change. That means we are the ones that are to be pro-active in bringing change about. However, in most cases the Christian community is the least likely to embrace change.

What is it that motivates people to change or to make changes in their lives? For most it is a desire to make things better, to improve life for themselves or for others. For others, change comes from a desire to relieve boredom, or is forced upon them by changes in their jobs or life circumstances.

What motivated Jesus? What motivated Peter, Paul, and the other saints of the New Testament to stand up against the defenders of the religious traditions of their day? For them it was more than just a desire for improvement. It was a passion that was rooted in their convictions. It has been said that not one person has ever died for his beliefs, although many have died for their convictions and passions. The missionaries who are martyred for their faith, the civil rights activists who are incarcerated for the stand they have taken, and the husbands and wives who lay down their lives for their families, all have one thing in common. Their beliefs had got hold of them, and changed them from fearful spectators to pro-active participants, whose convictions and passions enabled them to conquer their fear.

Due to the high levels of anxiety that are created when change is embarked upon, most Europeans have elected to put up with the old rather than risk the new. This is one reason why much of our culture is pre-occupied with preservation. We have become content with the old, not because we are convinced that it cannot be improved, but because it saves us from the fear, anxiety and uncertainty that embracing the new will bring.

Change is not easy. By nature we are creatures of habit that enjoy security and routine. But God has called us to a life of faith. For Peter, that meant stepping out of a boat, and onto a roaring sea. For us who knows? But unless we have a conviction, unless we are passionate about following Jesus, unless we are relentless in our search for Truth and are willing to put aside all the traditions and trappings of this world, we shall never be able to enter into the fullness of what God has bought for us by the blood of His own dear Son.

As Christians we differ from our unbelieving neighbors in one important aspect: whatever cultural assumptions we live by, we believe that the Scriptures are true un changeable, and a sure foundation on which to start building. With this sure foundation, we can then feel safe in questioning every other assumption by which we live. Had we lived in the days of Columbus, no doubt we all hope that we would have been courageous enough to listen to, and accept, the new theories about a round Earth.

Are we brave enough, today, to listen to, and perhaps accept the idea that our basic assumptions about the Church may not, in fact, be absolute or Biblically correct?

If so, then surely our love for God, and the desire to see His Kingdom expressed upon the earth, compels us to re-examine and re-evaluate our understanding of Church using Scripture alone as the final authority? As we do so, we may be surprised by what we find; for not only will we be confronted by centuries-old traditions, but also by a host of insecurities, fears, doubts and hopes, of which we have never previously been aware.

> *"Therefore, do not be conformed to the pattern of the world, but be transformed by the renewing of your mind that you may test and approve the good, acceptable, and perfect will of God." (Rom 12:2)*

Chapter 2

WHY ARE WE BUILDING THESE TOWERS?

"We know that we are of God and that the whole world lies in the power of the evil one" (**1 John. 5:19**)

Since the beginning of human history, people have been finding ways to structure and order society. This is good, since God is a God of order and not chaos. In the Garden of Eden there was order and structure. Adam and Eve were given work to do, and they related together in perfect harmony, as well as being in harmony with nature. Since the fall, however, different peoples in different lands have, over time, enveloped their unique cultures. These cultures provide a basis of common understanding and assumptions which enable people to live together in harmony. The cultural norms also provide means by which disputes can be settled, and the highly charged issues of money, sex, and power can be negotiated and contained. Rules lay out, for that society, the norms and expectations for morality, marriage, ownership, employment, government and so on.

On the whole, each society tries to create a system for itself that is self-sustaining and beneficial. But this is where the problems come in, for the question has to be asked, "beneficial for whom"? In the Garden, when everything was in harmony with God's Will there was no question but that the way it was ordered and run was beneficial to everyone man, woman, animals, and plants. But since the fall, without exception, we find that societies are full of corruption and biases that result in much benefit for a few, and much hardship for many.

Over the centuries Jews, and then Christians have recognized the deep iniquities in society and have tried to oppose and correct them. Although there has been some notable success, such as the abolition of slavery, one can only wonder why it took the Christian community many centuries to recognize that their own participation in slavery was wrong? Had Scripture changed, or was this blindness due to the influence of the prevailing culture? If so how do these principles affect us today?

Paul said *"Do not conform any longer to the pattern of this world"* (Rom 12:2a)

But just what is "the pattern of the world"? The Greek word for "world" in this verse is "kosmos" and it refers to order and arrangement. It includes everything that men have developed for the conduct and control of their societies, including every system of government, education, religion, economics, defense, finance, business and entertainment. As a result of the fall, all of these came under the dominion of Satan (Luke 4:6).

In the account of the Tower of Babel we read about Man's desire to "make a name for ourselves" (Gen 11:4). What we see is man trying to create a structure that will bring glory to himself rather than to God. Why would he do this? The answer goes right back to the fall when Satan tempted Eve with the possibility that she could be like God. In preferring her own wisdom to the wisdom of God, she chose the path of disobedience and set herself up as her own authority, in effect, taking the place of God himself.

> *"For God knows that in the day you eat of it your eyes will be opened, and you will be as God....And when the woman saw that the tree was good...and a tree to be desired to make one wise she took of its fruit and ate"* (Gen 3:5-6)

In that instance, she places herself at odds with God, and in submission to Satan, whom she had obeyed. And at that instant Satan became the ruler of this age (see Luke 4:6, Eph 2:2).

From that time on, Satan has been working through the hearts of men and women, motivating them to: oppose God's will; set themselves up as gods; and seek after their own glory making a name for themselves. And as we look at all the monuments to Man in society we can see how well he has succeeded in this! Furthermore, every individual is filled with the same spirit of selfishness seeking to make a name for himself or herself, not just collectively with others, but individually, "looking out for number one!"

This striving and struggling to meet our own needs without any real regard to the needs of others is the "pattern of the world", and is the "number one" destroyer of our relationships, both with God, and with one another. This is law of sin that Paul struggled with in Rom 7. It is the out-flowing of our own fallen human nature, energized by the principalities and powers that are ruled by Satan, the god of this age.

In the time of Noah, God was saddened and grieved by the depravity of Man. He sought out a handful of righteous men, and then destroyed everything else, thus giving Man a second chance. Yet, in no time at all, we find Man proudly building a monument to himself at Babel!

Throughout history, we have seen countless examples of unrighteous systems and organizations. Slavery and the domination of women are but two examples. Our concern is not with these specifics, but rather with the motivating spirit behind it all.

> *"For we struggle not against flesh and blood, but against the rulers, against the authorities, against the powers of this dark world and against the spiritual forces of evil in the heavenly realms."* (Eph 6:12)

These spiritual forces control and affect each one of us, whether we recognize it or not. In most cases we are not even aware of their effect, and yet they affect and largely determine the way we run our lives, our marriages, our finances, our businesses.

In the Scriptures, this system, this "pattern of the world", this willful disobedience, is referred to as Babylon, and is described and personified in Revelation.

> *"Then the angel carried me away in the Spirit into a desert. There I saw a woman sitting on a scarlet beast that was covered with blasphemous names and had seven heads and ten horns. The woman was dressed in purple and scarlet, and was glittering with gold, precious stones and pearls. She held a golden cup in her hand, filled with abominable things and the filth of her adulteries. This title was written on her forehead:*

MYSTERY
BABYLON THE GREAT
THE MOTHER OF PROSTITUTES
AND OF THE ABOMINATIONS OF THE EARTH"
(Rev 17:3-5)

"The woman you saw is the great city that rules over the kings of the earth." (Rev 17:18)

Scripture uses the name Babylon not just to refer to the physical earthly city, but also to the whole system - ethos - of society that she represents. In Revelation she is revealed as the city that rules over all aspects of worldly life - governments, commerce, leisure and families, etc.

This pattern of government became very evident when Satan enticed Man to selfishly "make a name" for himself by joining forces together to build a city and a tower that would reach the heavens. (Gen 11:4). Since that time, Satan has effectively infiltrated every aspect of human society so that almost every organization in the world is ruled by this spirit. The result is a characteristic structure that is used to bring "order" to almost every human organization. In fact it is so ingrained in our minds that we cannot conceive of any other way in which an organization could be structured.

Babylon is not just a pattern for organizational government, but rather a whole way of ordering society. It affects everything from kings and dictators down to the local chess club. Since its root is in fear and in selfishness, it is an abomination to the Lord! Please be very clear on this, when we, and the Scriptures, refer to Babylon, we are not only talking about the structures but about the principalities and powers that energize and motivate the structures. The actual structures - the Tower of Babel, slavery, domination of women, oppression of the poor, the abuse of power by the mighty, and so on - are all bad and worthy of condemnation. But they are only the symptoms of a deeper disease - the pernicious, pervasive power of the Babylonian spirit.

Please understand, however, that we are not condemning the need for organization or structure. God has organized the whole universe in a very structured way. But when God organizes, He does so with a motivation of love, and His structures produce life (just a quick look at Nature will demonstrate that). Our goal is to help you to "discern the spirits", (1 John 4:1) to recognize the presence of the destructive power of Babylon, even when it might be dressed up as something coming from an "angel of light" (2 Cor 11:14)

COME OUT OF HER MY PEOPLE

Paul said *"Do not conform any longer to the pattern of this world"* (Rom 12:2a)

A voice from heaven said *"Come out of her [Babylon], my people"* (Rev 18:4b)

And Jesus said *"You cannot serve both God and Mammon"* (Matt 6:24)

Satan is the ruling power of this age. His system for organizing the world, which we have identified as Babylon, permeates every aspect of society and produces a whole host of evil. As Christians, we usually have no difficulty in recognizing the evils that are so evident around us. Many of us, motivated by the grieving Spirit of God, have attempted to opposes these evils and bring change to the systems that have caused them. Usually we will try to do this by reorganizing the existing structures. We set in place checks, balances, accountability systems, and watchdog officials to ensure that the evils are righted so that the structures are more fair and less exploitive. The problem with this is that it does not confront the spirit of Babylon that is ruling these structures. Instead of releasing them from the devil's grip, all that we succeed in doing is to rearrange the systems so that we have a slightly different organization. It is still Babylon, just Babylon rearranged!

The Scriptures are very clear. We CANNOT reform anything that is energized by Babylon. Jesus was not a reformer. On an individual level He called people to be born again. The apostle Paul in 2Cor 5:17 states that, through being born again, one becomes a new creation. *"Old things have passed away [i.e. done away with, not reformed] behold all things have become new"*. On a corporate level the same principle applies. Jesus' mandate from the Father was not to reform the judicial system, which was merely an incomplete foretaste of the Kingdom of God. As we understand it, Jesus invested no time or energy seeking to bring improvements to this system. He is no more interested in perpetuating the man-made systems of religion today than He was then. In ancient Israel the leaders of the religious system made new converts "sons of hell" (Matt 23:15) in the name of God! Today little has changed.

In His earthly ministry Jesus publicly exposed to the common people the snares and abuses of Judaism so that they could come out of it and enter into the Kingdom of God. Today, institutional Christianity (with its man-made rules, paid professionals and rituals) has, for the believer, replaced Judaism in masquerading as the Kingdom of God. If we are to follow in the footsteps of the King, One who placed truth above tradition, then serious questions need to be asked about our own commitments. Just as we cannot be devoted to both Islam and Christianity, so we cannot be fully committed to Jesus and His Kingdom and at the same time be investing our time, money and energy into a system which has no eternal value. This is very clear from Jesus' declaration that we cannot serve two masters - "No one can serve two masters; for either he will hate the one and love the other, or else he will be loyal to the one and despise the other. You cannot serve God and mammon." (Matt 6:24).

Paul elaborates on this in 2 Tim 2:4: "No one engaged in warfare entangles himself with the affairs of this life, that he may please him who enlisted him as a soldier.".

Throughout Scripture we can see very clearly that God's method of dealing with sinful structures is to TOTALLY DESTROY them, not to try to renew, improve or reform them. The Flood was used to wipe out all of humanity so that God could start again with a righteous man. Sodom and Gomorrah was yet another example; Abraham pleaded with God to spare the cities for the sake of any righteous people in it, but God drew out the righteous and then flattened the city (Gen 18:16-33)!

In the New Testament, Christ's teaching is extremely clear: we must die before we can become righteous:

"Therefore pick up your cross and follow me" (Mark 8:34) *"Everyone who is in Christ is a new creation, the old has gone the new has come"* (2 Cor:17) *"Since you died with Christ to the basic principles of this world, why, as though you still belonged to it, do you submit to its rules?"* (Col 2:20) God is not interested in preserving the structures we have set up. He is interested only in drawing people to Himself and into His righteousness. God destroyed the Temple at Jerusalem since it represented a system and structure that was made redundant through the death of Christ. No longer would worship occur in a man-made temple, instead it would occur in temples of flesh - the bodies of those of us who have died and been born again. "It is no longer I who lives, but Christ that lives within me." (Gal 2:20) No longer do we require human priests, since now we are all priests with Jesus as our high priest. (1 Pet 2:9).

It is futile trying to change, renew or improve structures that are inherently oppressive and destructive, and are in fact tools of the enemy. God's solution is always to clear the slate and to start afresh. This is in direct contrast to the religions of man that seek to start with what exists and then make it better. This should not be surprising, since those systems are energized by the spirit of Babylon who would have no desire to tear down the structure to replace it with something more righteous!

Chapter 3

THE KINGDOM OF DARKNESS

God is a God of order, not of chaos. He has created the Universe to follow strict laws, and He has created us also to be part of this order. As Creator He is, of course, the Supreme Authority and, at the appointed time, everything and everyone in creation must, and will, submit to this Authority.

When God created Mankind, however, He delegated some of this authority to man, charging him to rule over the Earth (Gen 1:28). In this manner, and for as long as man ruled in accordance with the will of God, the Kingdom of God would be manifest on Earth. Unfortunately, as we know, this situation did not last for long. In disobeying God, man usurped His authority, and in obeying Satan's suggestions, man handed over his God given authority to Satan.

> *"They exchanged the truth of God for a lie, and worshipped and served created things rather than the Creator"* (Rom 1:25).

> "... you were dead in your transgressions and sins, in which you used to live when you followed the ways of this world and of the ruler of the kingdom of the air, the spirit who is now at work in those who are disobedient. All of us also lived among them at one time, gratifying the cravings of our sinful nature and following its desires and thoughts." (Eph 2:1-3) "...
>
> The whole world is under the control of the evil one." (1 John 5:19).

In this way Satan was enthroned as the "god of this age" and we became subjects not of the Kingdom of God (i.e. living under the active rule of God), but of the Kingdom of Satan, also known as the Kingdom of Darkness. Of course God is still ultimately in control, all authority ultimately comes from Him, and we will ultimately be accountable before Him. But in delegating authority to Man, He has allowed us to have enormous latitude in structuring our society according to our perceptions of what is right.

This delegation, and its abdication by us to Satan, has had enormous repercussions affecting every aspect of human society, including the church. As we shall see, our minds have become so conditioned by Satan's concepts of government, that, not only is our social and business life corrupted by it, but so also is almost every expression of God's Church on Earth! To fully understand this, we need to first examine how the Kingdom of Darkness operates, and then we will contrast this with the Kingdom of Light, God's Kingdom, and how that operates.

What Motivates Man?

> "Everything in the world - the cravings of sinful man, the lust of his eyes and the boasting of what he has

and does - comes not from the Father but from the world" (1 John 2:16).

The underlying basis to fallen, sinful, society is FEAR, and the primary instinct of its members is SELFISH to achieve our own ambitions, to satisfy our own desires.

As unredeemed people, cut off from the security and love of God, we are full of fears and insecurities; fear of failure and fear of rejection being chief among them. Motivated by these, and also by desires for sensual pleasures we strive after the four "G's" Girls, Guys, Gold, and Glory, or in other words:

MONEY

In all but perhaps the poorest of peasant societies the desire to acquire possessions, to own things, and in particular to own more things than others is the norm. For the sake of money, people will lie, cheat, steal, and even kill. It is rare to find someone who is content with what he has, and who is not searching for ways to have more, or similarly, to have the same but with less work!

SEX

The search for sexual pleasures is rampant throughout all societies through the ages, and fuels an enormous industry in the West. For example, advertising, cosmetics, magazines, clothing fashions, music, and now films all use sex as a selling point. On an individual level, it is a preoccupation of many adults, and has led to countless divorces and scandals both in and out of the church.

FAME & POWER

Not only do these give us the ability to achieve more of the above two, but in them we also look for an antidote to our fears of rejection and failure. Surely if we are famous and powerful then that means that we cannot be failures and that people *do* like us? To achieve such positions of influence we will trample over others, manipulate them, and even sell our bodies in exchange for advancement.

Please note that we have ALL lived in this way to some extent (Rom 1:10-12). Indeed, even as redeemed believers, we continue to struggle against these desires as we seek to have our minds renewed and our hearts purified (James 1:14-15).

> "Love not the world, neither the things [that are] in the world. If any man love the world, the love of the Father is not in him. For all that [is] in the world, the lust of the flesh, and the lust of the eyes, and the pride of life, is not of the Father, but is of the world." (1 John 2:15-16).

Because of our fears and our selfishness, society becomes a battleground in which we all strive to fulfill our sinful ambitions (Jas 4:1). At times we will co-operate with each other, when this seems to be to our advantage. At other times we will do whatever is necessary to eliminate those that are our rivals or that seem to stand in our way. In this dog-eats-dog world, those that are the most powerful will rise to the top and exert their power over others in order to use others for their own gain.

Worldly Authority

> Jesus called them together and *said "You know that the rulers of the Gentiles lord it over them, and their high officials exercise authority over them."* (Matt. 20:25).

In some situations this use of power is crude and obvious. Examples include gangster organizations such as the Mafia, and military dictators who dominate whole countries. In other situations it is much more subtle. In business, for example, the goal is to rise to the top of the corporate ladder, to become a manager with a fancy office, expensive car, large salary, and power over numerous employees who have to be polite lest they are given the sack!

The inevitable result of this, and indeed the hallmark of the Kingdom of Darkness is a pyramidal structure of authority and control that looks like this:

Chief Executive Officer
(i.e. the Boss, President, Founder, Owner)

Senior Management
(i.e. those responsible for carrying out the orders of the Boss)

Junior Management
(i.e. those answerable to senior management)

Workers
(i.e. those who actually do the work of the organization)

Note:
1) There is just one person (or possibly a small group of people) at the top, and each level below has increasing numbers of people.
2) The authority that each level has is delegated from above, and is based on their ability to control the things that are important to the level below (e.g. wages, opportunity for promotion). In other words,

the submission of each level is based on their fear of what their boss could do (e.g. cut wages, demote, fire) and also their greed for the things their boss can offer them (e.g. promotion, pay rise, public recognition). See, for example, the Roman commander's concern at mistakenly and illegally imprisoning a Roman citizen in Acts 22:26-29 and also Pilate's expectation that his power over Jesus should be a motivator for Jesus to be co-operative in John 19:10.

3) Every person in each level tries to produce the best work using the resources of those beneath him, so that he can best impress his boss and therefore seek advancement ahead of his colleagues. Often this competition between employees is explicitly encouraged, in order to get each one working harder.

4) At each level the managers have little interest in the concerns of those employees below them, except in as much as it affects the usefulness of the employees to the organization. In other words, a good manager will do all that he can to make his employees happy and well trained, since this will make them more productive, and this in turn will reflect well on the manager and his own chances for advancement.

As you read these statements you can no doubt think of some companies that very clearly display such a cold, calculating environment. But you may also be wondering about some of the modern firms that work hard at providing a caring, supportive and nurturing environment for their employees. The message of these companies would appear to be "we care about you and want the best for you". But a closer analysis will still reveal the same principles described above. The ultimate goal is still to make money for the owners, the workers are still the means by which such profit will be made, and the culture of the company, with all its warmth and support, is specifically designed to be that way because it does actually produce better productivity than a harsh climate. However warm and friendly everyone seems, people are still eager for advancement and fearful of redundancy. In large companies the work force are often referred to as "human resources" which would seem to place them alongside other assets such as "physical resources", "financial resources" etc. Finally, relationships among colleagues are almost exclusively task based, especially when these relationships are vertical (i.e. manager and worker) rather than horizontal (manager to manager or worker to worker). Whilst the company may encourage social outings in order to promote a team spirit, how many of these relationships continue after an employee has left the firm? The one exception to this is the office romance - and that, when it is a vertical relationship, is notoriously complicated as it interferes with the normal running of the firm which is based on the above hierarchical principles.

However all this is in conflict with Scripture which teaches us to work "as unto the Lord".

On your second reading we would suggest that you stop at this point and spend some time praying and meditating about the things you have read and how they apply to you. The following questions may help you in this process:

1) We have all heard and used the term "hasn't he done well for himself?" when talking about people who have prospered in their jobs and careers. From your understanding of Christ's teaching in the sermon on the Mount (Matt 5), what do you think Jesus would think about such a statement?
2) Do you think that the phrase "hasn't he done well for others?" would be more in line with Christ's teaching?

3) List the areas in your life in which you are seeking to do well for yourself. Are you happy with these priorities? Are there any changes that need to be made to bring them in line with the priorities of God's Kingdom?
4) Does the "church" that you attend on Sunday have a structure that looks anything like that which we have listed above? If so, does it bother you, or should it bother you?

Chapter 4

THE CHURCH IN BABYLON

Having looked at the manifestation of Babylon in our secular society, we now turn our attention to the structures and institutions that we call "church". As "new creations" in Christ have we been able to escape the influence of Babylon as we have organized and structured our Christian fellowship? Or have we fallen into the same pit as the rest of the world? Has the "church", as we have organized it, simply become another manifestation of Babylon? Many of us have invested years of our lives, and thousands of dollars into these "churches". We therefore tend to be very protective of them "for where your treasure is, there your heart will be also" (Matt 6:21). Furthermore, we have repeatedly been taught not to be critical or judgmental. But if we are to be genuine seekers of truth and righteousness we cannot avoid asking these questions, however painful they might be.

Unfortunately, if we look around us with open eyes, we will be horrified to see the footprint of Babylon in our "churches", both now, and throughout history.

The spirit of the world is manifest in all its ugliness in the "churches" which glory in the size of their buildings, their numbers of members, their wealth and their programs. It can be seen in the man- oriented services, the preaching aimed at impressing or entertaining audiences, the music and singing, and the star performers in theatre type situations, which are often no more than "show-biz" dressed up in Christian wrappings.

The institutional "church" has rejected God's government, and set itself up with hierarchies of Popes, Bishops, Priests, and other "clergy" ruling over groups of leaders called synods, councils, or presbyteries, who then rule over individual churches with their priests, vicars, pastors, or ministers, who rule over their body of elders and deacons, who rule over the congregation or "laity". Over the past 2000 years we have "denominated" (i.e. made a name for) ourselves into over 40,000 different organizations, each with a man-made name, each competing, each claiming to have a better understanding of the "Truth".

Within each "church" it would appear that the chief goal is to add more members who will agree with our own doctrines and who will thus become our members rather than members of a competing church. We try to attract such new members by putting on "enjoyable and meaningful" worship services that have more to do with entertaining the masses than with pleasing God. Countless courses and seminars are offered on how to improve our lives "in Christ" in order to be more prosperous, happy, or secure, yet there is almost no discipleship training to equip and empower Christians to pour out their lives for others. Not only that, but the global Church currently spends in excess of 95% of its income on itself and less than 0.5% on taking the gospel to those still outside the promises and blessings of the new covenant, the very ones that are most on God's heart. With statistics like this it is hard to pat ourselves on the back for a job well done! Sadly we seem to have lost our way. It seems that much of what we now do has more to do with the meeting of our own needs, ambitions, and desires, than it has with God's global plan. In many ways the church has simply become a social club. What is more, our attempts at religion are a stench in the nostrils of our Lord:

> "*You do not delight in sacrifice, or I would bring it; you do not take pleasure in burnt offerings. The sacrifices of God are a broken spirit; a broken and contrite heart, O God you will not despise.*" (Ps 51:16-17).

Babylon is as alive and active in our "churches" as it is in the Mafia and every other aspect of society.

The leadership of such churches also has more to do with the ambitions and insecurities of the leaders than with service to the Lord and His people. If this is not the case, then how do we explain the following:-

1. Special Titles

Terms such as (bishop, priest, vicar, pastor, clergy, reverend) mark out the leader as being special, different and perhaps even superior to the ordinary people who are given the unbiblical label "the laity". This practice of dividing the Church into the clergy and laity is the very practice of the Nicolaitans that God despises in Rev 2:6 and 2:15. Some of these terms, such as pastor and bishop, are indeed Biblical, but are being used in a non-Biblical and destructive manner. The Biblical usage of these terms is discussed in detail later on in Chapter 9.

2. Special Clothes

The historical reasons for the robes and clerical collars are explored in chapter 7. In this day and age their only purpose is, once again, to set the person apart as being different to the ordinary folks - in other words, to accord him a special status.

3. Concerns about "Sheep Stealing"

At times we hear of a leader complaining that another "minister" is "sheep stealing". The use of the word "stealing" implies that this person is taking away something that does not belong to him but actually belongs to someone else. But do the people "belong" to one "minister" or another? And why would he get upset about people transferring from his "church" to another unless it in some way threatens what he values - such as the size of his congregation, the reputation of his ministry, or the size of his offerings? Since there is no biblical support for the concept of owning a congregation (see later chapters), it is difficult to come to any conclusion other than that such accusations of sheep stealing (and indeed the practice of sheep stealing) are motivated by the Babylonian spirit of personal ambition and empire-building.

Yet in many cases congregations themselves are not free of blame, since in paying their leader a stipend or salary they have effectively made him their "hired man". It has been our experience that those in such congregations in most cases will not speak out for fear of the animosity and division that will undoubtedly arise to what is, in most cases, interpreted as insubordination.

> "As He taught, Jesus said, 'Watch out for the teachers of the law. They like to walk around in flowing robes and be greeted in the market-places, and have the most important seats in the synagogues ("churches") and the places of honor at banquets. They devour widows' houses and for a show make lengthy prayers. Such men will be punished most severely.'"
> (Mark 12:38-40).

Please note that we do not reject the need for leadership, but the Godly pattern for leadership, which we discuss later in the book, is very, very different from the Babylonian hierarchies we have just been describing.

Restricting normal growth

Sadly, the established church has not only failed miserably in helping its members to mature and become disciples. It has in fact actively prevented people from growing! Later on we shall see the underlying reasons why. At this point, however, we will just look at how.

As Paul says, "We have much to say about this, but it is hard to explain because you are slow to learn. In fact, though by this time you ought to be teachers, you need someone to teach you the elementary truths of God's word all over again. You need milk, not solid food! Anyone who lives on milk, being still an infant, is not acquainted with the teaching about righteousness. But solid food is for the mature who, by constant use, have trained themselves to distinguish good from evil" (Heb 5:11-14). The writer to the Hebrews was horrified that so many in the Church were still so immature. When we are born again into the family of God we are spiritual babies. But the expectation is that we should grow up.

"Brothers stop thinking like children. In regard to evil be infants, but in your thinking be adults" (1 Cor 14:20)

"It was He who gave some to be apostles, some to be prophets, some to be evangelists, and some to be pastors and teachers, to prepare God's people for works of service, so that the body of Christ may be built up until we all reach unity in the faith and in the knowledge of the Son of God and become mature, attaining to the whole measure of Christ. Then we will no longer be infants, tossed back and forth by the waves, and blown here and there by every wind of

teaching and by the cunning and craftiness of men in their deceitful scheming. Instead, speaking the truth in love, we will, in all things, grow up into Him who is the Head, that is Christ. From Him the whole body, joined and held together by every supporting ligament, grows and builds itself up in love, as each part does its work." Eph 4:11-15

We are called to be disciples whose daily passion is to be more like Jesus. It is our responsibility to "work out our salvation with fear and trembling" until we reach maturity. We are to be seekers after the truth, for it is in the seeking that we shall find, and it is only then that we will become overcomers who are "more than conquerors". God will provide us with many mature role models from whom we can learn. He will also provide us with good and bad experiences, all of which will "work together for the good of those who love God [i.e. those who obey His commands]" (Rom 8:28). But it is we who must make use of all of these in order to grow.

Masses dominated by the educated

Right through history there have always been those who dominated and those who were dominated. In most cases those who were dominated were those who were uneducated and unaware of their rights. Therefore, once the masses have been educated in regard to their rights, the days are numbered for those who use their knowledge to control others. This gives those who have knowledge, and with it power, a massive incentive to withhold that knowledge from the masses so that they cannot rise up and take over the power. This may sound like Marxism, but is in fact a truth that applies as much too institutional churches as to secular societies.

Second Class Citizens

The Church of today is divided into the professionals or clergy, and the ordinary believers or laity. Along with this distinction is the strong implication that the clergy are in some way better or more holy Christians than the ordinary man or woman in the pew. After all, the reasoning is that the minister (or priest, vicar, pastor, bishop, elder) is in full-time ministry and I am just an ordinary person in a secular job, so a value judgment is made. There are things that the "ordinary believer" cannot or should not do, things that need to be left to the "professionals". This system is largely to blame for the general lack of maturity within the body of Christ, and unfortunately has bound up countless millions of good honest Christians who have felt discouraged and useless, turning the average local group of believers into spectators and passive pew-warmers.

Three Case Histories

1) Several years ago we were asked to meet with the leadership team of a large and influential Anglican Church in London, England. Our brief for this evening meeting was to conduct a test seeking to discover the balance and distribution of gifts amongst those in the leadership team of six men and one woman. The test which we used asks a series of 35 questions *(see the "must read" article on Motivational Gifts)* that require an honest self-rating, on a scale of 1-10, of what one would do in certain situations. At the end of the test each participant is asked to add up their scores, and these scores, when related to the graph enclosed with the test, gives a very accurate picture of one's gifts and their relative strengths. What was discovered, to the horror of the full-time vicar, was that everyone in the leadership group, without exception, had a broader base of gifts than him. In

fact the vicar himself scored the lowest of all on the leadership dimension. From that moment onwards, the vicar began to manifest insecurity and control, which became instantly recognizable to the others who had participated in the test. The outcome of this was that within three months the leadership team was disbanded, more than 350 people left the church, and the vicar came under discipline from the Bishop. The saddest situation of all in this case was that the vicar did not need to come under "church discipline". What he needed was to be released from his "job" so that he could discover and develop the many gifts that God had placed within him.

2) Another example is Alan (not his real name), who works as the personnel officer for the international office of a large UK bank. As you can imagine, with about 3000 employees located in one place, Alan finds himself very busy. He helps staff members with their financial problems, offers counsel and guidance to those going through divorce, offers wisdom and care to those experiencing emotional trauma, helps new employees to settle into their area, supports those who are struggling. All in all, Alan is a pastor. He is gifted as one, and he is functioning as one. However, should you ask Alan whether or not he is a pastor, his reply would be "No! I work for the bank." You see, Alan does not recognize that what he is doing is his full-time ministry in the Lord's service! Alan has been deceived by a Babylonian system into thinking that what he is doing is neither as spiritual nor as valuable as that of the professional "minister".

3) Take John, for instance (not his real name). Wanting to be more effective in his service for the Lord, he was told that Bible School was the doorway to ministry and therefore he should seek to be "trained in the

Word" with a view to entering "full-time ministry". What nonsense! As a committed believer he already is in "full-time ministry". Interestingly, the New Testament does not once mention the concept of "full-time ministry", since the role of priest and keeper of the Temple was ended at the Cross. Therefore, ministry has to do with what God has deposited in us (gifts, love, mercy, service, etc), and its overflow into the world about us. Contrast this with the Babylonian churches that teach, by example, that ministry is a job for which you can be trained and employed, irrespective of the gifts and abilities placed in you by God. The evidence of this is that many denominations require candidates to have a Bible School degree before they can be appointed to a paid job as a "minister".

When he graduated, instead of entering "the ministry", John felt led to take up a job in a big telecommunications company. But, as he did so, he was mocked by the other students who thought he should go into a proper "full-time ministry" (i.e. become a "pastor" or other church leader). John stuck to his convictions, but on meeting him several years later we found him to be feeling discouraged and sidelined. Struggling with low self-esteem he continued to doubt himself. He wondered if indeed he had settled for "second best", as his classmates had earlier indicated. John, in his ministry among unbelievers at his work place, is as much in full-time ministry as any "pastor" and is probably a lot more effective in bringing the Kingdom to a lost and hurting world! It is for people like John that this book has been written.

Despite the discouragement John has felt, we should probably give thanks to God that he was not seduced into following the career paths of his peers into the Babylonian church. Had he done so, this is what would almost certainly have happened:

(a) After graduating, he would have done a year as an "intern" or assistant pastor in an established "church". He would have learned the duties and responsibilities of maintaining an organization preparing sermons, doing pastoral visits, managing staff and overseeing budgets.

One of John's first priorities in his new position would be to impress both his congregation and his boss (the senior pastor). No one would admit to this, but this is essential if, after the internship, he is to get some good job offers.

(b) After the training year, John would then, hopefully, receive a "call" from a "church" that is looking for a new pastor. They would interview him, and examine the record of his achievements during his training year. If he had been outspoken and prophetic, challenging the complacencies and hypocrisies of the Babylonian system, then his chances of securing a full time appointment would be slim. Therefore it is in John's best interests to conform during this training year.

(c) Once he is in a definitive Pastor's position John's troubles would really begin. What would be expected of John in his full-time salaried position would have little or nothing to do with who John is as an individual, or with the gifts that the Lord has deposited within him. For example, if John has a strong gift of evangelism, with a desire to get out into the world to reach the lost, he might easily find himself very frustrated with the demands that would be placed upon him if the previous "minister" had set up structures for extensive pastoral care to those that are already "members of the church". Furthermore, if John does not have the gifts of leadership (Rom 12:3-8), how could he be expected to lead the congregation? It would be fair to say at this point that, in our experience of hundreds of "churches", most men who accept these positions of leadership are in fact not anointed leaders, but trained managers.

(d) As the "pastor", John would be expected to provide wise counsel and ministry to people of both sexes, from all walks of life, and of all ages. The assumption is that since John has been trained in counseling skills, he must therefore be competent and effective at the job. This flies in the face of the Biblical teaching that different people have been gifted and anointed in different ways (see Rom 12:3-13). John may indeed be anointed with godly wisdom as a counselor, in which case he will do the task well. But what if he has no such anointing? How can the seminary training be expected to turn him into something that he is not?

(e) However much he might declare that he is not interested in numbers, John would have no option but to watch very carefully the numerical growth or decline of his congregation. This is because it reflects on two issues:

i) There is an assumption that, if numbers are going up, then the church (and particularly the pastor) must be doing things right, whereas if the numbers decrease, then something must be wrong (perhaps the quality of the preaching, an un-welcoming environment, poor music, etc. etc). As the man in charge, this will all reflect on John.

ii) In most cases the number of members determines the amount of income received through "tithes and offerings". Since most "churches" have significant financial obligations, the number of people walking through the doors has a critical bearing on whether the bills get paid. If the numbers go down, John would be in big trouble, and may not even get his own salary paid!

So, if John is to protect his family and ensure that he is secure in his job, he must continue to conform to the expectations of the system. How can he dare to preach a radical gospel that confronts people's comfortable lifestyles when this may then result in people becoming offended and leaving the "church"? By this time John is trapped, and has little option but to continue to perpetuate Babylon. "For the time will come when men will not put up with sound doctrine, but according to their own desires because they have itching ears, they will heap up for themselves teachers; and they will turn their ears away from the truth and be turned aside to fables." (2 Tim 4:3-4).

After extensive research and numerous in-depth studies of the New Testament, we can find not one shred of evidence to support this destructive and binding model that the masses have been told is church.

This is the "yeast of the Pharisees and Sadducees" (Matt 16:5-12) against which Jesus warned His disciples. Like the Pharisees, the leaders of the Babylonian church will "travel over land and sea to win a single convert, and when he becomes one, you make him twice as much a son of hell as you are." (Matt 23:15). Remember that Jesus was saying this to the religious leaders - those who were supposedly zealous for God and for obedience to His Word. Satan uses many tactics to keep people out of the Kingdom of God, but his most effective is his most subtle: to set up a parallel system, a counterfeit system, that looks so close to the real thing that nearly everyone is deceived into thinking that it is the real thing! Please understand that we are not judging the individual, we are speaking out against the Babylon system that calls itself church.

Asking questions

As one reads the Scripture, it is clear that Jesus spent a great deal of His time asking questions. In most instances the questions He asked would reveal men's hearts and motives. Today, within the institutional church, questions with regard to why we do things are perceived as a threat, and truth seeking believers are discarded, sidelined and avoided as trouble-makers. It is this issue that convinces us that most of the modern day institutional denominations are more committed to the traditions in their organizations than to the truth of the New Testament.

When faced with an environment that discourages truth-seeking, believers such as John have three choices - to keep quiet, speak up, or leave. If they keep quiet, they are permitted to remain within the organized structure called church. As a result they are still accepted, have social contact, and are told that they are being faithful to God. But all of this comes at the cost of deep frustration, poor self esteem, and confusion. They know that God has given them gifts and abilities, so why are they not allowed to use them? They have a genuine desire to minister to others, so why are only the elders allowed to do so?

Alternatively they can choose to speak up: Why does the pastor do all the teaching? Why is the money spent on buildings and salaries instead of being given to the poor? Why do Christians pretend to be happy all the time, when in fact many of them have deep hurts and needs for which they need ministry? Such questions would quickly upset the ordered, organized functioning of the "church" organization, and anyone asking them may find himself quietly ignored or publicly excluded from the assembly as a troublemaker. Suddenly all the people whom he once regarded as his friends seem to disappear, lest they also be tainted by their association with him!

Maturity through Participation

The apostle Paul asks in 1 Cor 14:26 *"How is it then, brethren, whenever you come together each of you has a psalm, has a teaching, has a tongue, has a revelation, has an interpretation. Let all things be done for edification"*.

The New Testament Church is a body where each member plays his/her part. Contrast his with today's "church" suffocated with non-biblical traditions and paid professionals and it is no wonder what the "church" would seem unrecognizable to the early Christians. With spectator-style congregations being dominant across the globe, it is hardly surprising that the Church has failed to impart the message of the gospel to a hurting world.

Low self esteem

With a mixture of low self-esteem, a lack of Biblical knowledge and fear, the institutional church has deceived the masses into accepting a form of "church" that the early apostles would hardly recognize. For those who have their security based in the traditions of men rather than the word of God, the step towards discovering the truth in regard to the New Testament Church will be a step they are unwilling to take. Their low self-esteem and fear of rejection paralyses them into silence. If we are to see the hurting, the rejected and the wounded coming into a place of security and worth in Jesus, then radical steps will need to be taken.

The attractive whore

In its most blatant form, such as with dictators, Babylon is crude and repulsive, and is quickly denounced by most people. But Satan is a master of lies, deceptions, and counterfeits *"and no wonder, for Satan himself masquerades as an angel of light"* (2 Cor 11:14). He dresses up the whore, Babylon, so that she is pretty and attractive - adorned in gold, silver, and jewels. In this way we are sucked into her deception.

This is exactly where we, the church, have fallen into the deception. A well run "church" that has a beautiful, comfortable building, and that is constantly adding new members, feels so "right". We feel accepted by friendly members (thus addressing one of our basic needs) and, if we follow the rules and join all the right activities, we can even be promoted to become a deacon or elder. We have pious "services" in which we join together to "worship God", and we listen attentively to the minister as he reads from "The Word of God" and then lectures us on how we can be better Christians. How can this not be pleasing to God?

But what if we question any of the church's (manmade) traditions, or why so much money is being spent on a building? What if, in obedience to Christ's commands, we dare to baptize someone without the pastor's consent? Then we will, in most cases, be quickly shunned and branded as "rebels" who have seriously and sadly lost our way! If we cannot be "won back" into conformity, then we will in most cases be thrown out or rejected as a dangerous influence on the rest of the congregation. Of course, all of this will be done in the Name of the Lord, and in the interests of maintaining the purity of doctrine and the safety of the congregation.

Thus the "church" ensures obedience and submission, not by our love for God, but through our fear of the leadership and others and what they might do if we step out of line.

On your second reading we would suggest that you stop at this point and spend some time praying and meditating about the things you have read and how they apply to you. The following questions may help you in this process:

1) How much of your thinking, in regard to Christian issues, is being shaped by the structures described above?
2) By whom, was Jesus mostly persecuted, and what was it that He said or did that made Him such a threat to the systems of the day?
3) If Jesus were here today in person, what do you think He may have to say in regard to the religious systems that have been erected in His name, and how do you think the "church" leaders of today would respond to His comments?
4) How do you imagine that your Home Group or Christian "friends" might respond, if you began to share with them, in an open time of fellowship, some of the issues that you are learning from this book?

Chapter 5

THE KINGDOM OF LIGHT

Through Jesus, God has *"rescued us from the Kingdom of Darkness and brought us into the Kingdom of the Son He loves"* (Col 1:15).

"This is how we know what love is: Jesus Christ laid down His life for us. And we ought to lay down our lives for our brothers. If anyone has material possessions and sees his brother in need, but has no pity on him, how can the love of God be in him?" (1 John 3:16-17).

"There is no fear in love. But perfect love drives out fear, because fear has to do with punishment." (1 John 4:18).

As we become believers and disciples of Christ, we once again find ourselves subjects in a Kingdom and we must submit to the King as the highest authority. But in this Kingdom the underlying basis is LOVE and the primary purpose of its subjects is SELFLESS: to bring glory to God and to help others to achieve their goals.

It is the exact opposite of the Kingdom of Darkness; the two kingdoms are absolutely incompatible, for we cannot serve two masters.

> *"But Jesus called them [to Him], and saith unto them, Ye know that they which are accounted to rule over the Gentiles exercise lordship over them; and their great ones exercise authority upon them. But so shall it not be among you: but whosoever will be great among you, shall be your minister: And whosoever of you will be the chiefest, shall be servant of all. For even the Son of Man came not to be ministered unto, but to minister, and to give His life as a ransom for many."* (Mark 10:42-45).

Jesus is, of course, our prime example of how the Kingdom of God operates. Jesus has all authority, granted by God Himself (Matt 28:18), and yet see how He uses that authority! Since He has no ambitions for Himself, He does not need to boss anyone around or manipulate them to do His bidding. He is not interested in building up a large following, and so He has no need to appease the masses or to pander to their selfish and carnal desires. Indeed He criticizes them for following Him just because He works miracles that feed, heal, and amaze them (John 6:26). Jesus focuses on two things only: on speaking the Truth; and on loving the people, making Himself available to them in any way that He can that would lead to their growing in genuine faith and love for God. At times this means harsh words of conviction. At other times it means tender ministrations of compassion, but at all times it is motivated by His desire to see others experience more of God's grace. When calling on people to follow Him, He did not use enticements or manipulation, they followed of their own free will, because they recognized God's anointing on Him (see Peter's confession in John 6:68).

Authority

From the discussions in the last two chapters we suggest that there are two opposing concepts of authority, of which one leads to bondage and the other leads to liberty:

Worldly authority is rooted in fear. Those in authority (by virtue of the power they wield) tell those under them what to do and what not to do, ultimately aiming to benefit themselves through the relationship. (See Previous Chapter) Those in submission do so out of fear and insecurity, and are afraid to think for themselves or to act except within the clear limits set up from above. Stepping outside those limits is risky and is rarely attempted without first seeking permission, or ensuring that the security is provided in some other way. Although not spelt out explicitly, the assumption that underlies the working practices of most local churches is that there are five levels of authority to which we must submit. In decreasing order these are:

1) The Scriptures (as understood and interpreted by the leadership and denomination). This is most clearly demonstrated by the rigid adherence to one or other side of the infant baptism issue.
2) God the Father, Son and Holy Spirit.
3) The advice, instruction and admonishment of the church leaders.
4) Your own conscience.
5) Other Christians and secular authority.

Please understand that no-one would intentionally relegate God to second place, for everyone's sincere desire would be to serve God with all their mind, heart and strength. The trouble is that, although they start off with honest intentions, the snares of Babylon quickly entrap them so that, in practice, the order of priorities becomes as listed above. This is most clearly shown by the heated debate, animosity and suspicion that often occurs between different "churches" or different denominations, despite Christ's clear command to "love one another". The desire to validate their understanding of Scripture has come before their obedience to God.

Godly authority is rooted in love. Since Love does not seek to control or manipulate, but only to build us up so that we may be more like Jesus, you will not find God's anointed leaders trying to enforce their authority over you. Instead, they will only have authority over you in as much as you voluntarily place yourself in submission to them. Instead of telling you what to do, such leaders will be encouraging you to think through problems for yourself so that you can work out for yourself what you should do. There are therefore not five, but four levels of authority:

1) God the Father, Son and Holy Spirit.
2) The Scriptures as you understand them (but be very careful how you interpret them, for you are answerable to the Lord).
3) Your own conscience (assuming of course it is being renewed and enlightened by the Holy Spirit).
4) Other Christians, and secular authority.

As you can see, this puts the responsibility on each of us to diligently seek after the Lord ("seek ye first the kingdom of God"). It also means that it is our responsibility to seek out those mature Christians whom we trust and who are able to provide us with wise counsel, as we seek to walk with God. The early believers "devoted themselves to the apostles' teaching" (Acts 2:42), and in the same way it is the responsibility of every believer to be a "seeker of the truth", taking every opportunity to ask questions and to learn more, rather than expecting some teacher to spoon feed us with what they think we need to know. As you can see, this is the exact opposite of what happens in almost every organized "church".

The Scriptures instruct us to place ourselves in submission. "Obey them that have the rule over you, and submit yourselves: for they watch for your souls, as they that must give account, that they may do it with joy, and not with grief: for that [is] unprofitable for you." (Heb 13:17) However, that submission is given by us to those godly men and women that we trust; confident that their counsel is unbiased and without any hidden agendas. We must be very careful that we do not place ourselves in submission to leaders (however holy they may sound) who are under the influence of Babylon since this will only stagnate our growth to maturity. What other reason can there be to explain why almost every "church" is populated almost exclusively by immature Christians?

On your second reading we would again suggest that you stop at this point and spend some time praying and meditating about the things you have read and how they apply to you. The following questions may help you in this process:

1) On a daily basis, which Kingdom has the greater influence on your actions? Do you tend to do things based on how they will bless others, without regard for how they will affect you, or are you more concerned about defending and advancing your own finances, position or reputation in the eyes of men?
2) Are you happy with your answer to question 1? If not, what holds you back from changing?

Chapter 6

THE HOUSE CHURCH / CELL GROUP MOVEMENT

Satan is the master of deception and sets himself up as an angel of light to deceive people into thinking they are serving God when in fact they are bound up by the devil. The house church movement is perhaps his most clever and pernicious deception so far. But before you bombard us with objections, please hear us out on this! We do not condemn individual leaders or members of house or cell groups. Most of these genuinely love the Lord and are doing the very best they can to be faithful to Him, based on the understanding and revelation they have. The cell group movement has been a blessing to millions, and has been the means by which many have been introduced to Jesus. We ourselves have been both members and leaders of house churches, and vigorously defended them as the solution to the problems of institutional Christianity. Yet at the same time, it has also brought many into a new kind of bondage. Let us look at this from the beginning:

Over the past two or three decades, many people have become increasingly disillusioned with the evident problems of the established institutional "churches": The "services" are too formal and restrictive; there is no freedom for people to participate, or to exercise their own gifts. There is no opportunity for people to become leaders, unless they go through the seminary route. It was recognized that God has called his people to be a community of people who relate to each other: sharing their joys and struggles, their testimonies and their prayer needs, and reaching out to their friends and neighbors to bring them into the Kingdom.

In order for these things to be happening, people need to be meeting in smaller groups, in their homes, work places, or any other convenient locations (e.g. restaurant, pub, beach, hotel), sharing together, praying together, worshipping together. This, of course, is very Biblical.

The problem comes when you try to make this happen.

> In the early church, the disciples, full of the life and the love of the Spirit, *"devoted themselves to the apostles' teaching and to the fellowship, to the breaking of bread and to prayer. Everyone was filled with awe, and many wonders and signs were done by the apostles. All the believers were together and had everything in common. Selling their possessions and goods, they gave to anyone as he had need. Every day they continued to meet together in the temple courts. They broke bread in their homes and ate together with glad and sincere hearts, praising God and enjoying the favor of all the people. And the Lord added to their number daily those who were being saved."* (Acts 2:42-47).

The crucial thing to notice is that no-one told them that this is what they were supposed to do! All that they did, they did freely and naturally because of the outpouring of the Love and the Life that Jesus had put in them, and their desire to obey His commands and imitate His lifestyle. In other words, the structure, or form, of their behavior (meeting in homes, sharing possessions etc) was a result of the life within them. This provides us with a very important principle:

The LIFE must come first, and will then lead to the FORM.

Unfortunately the house church, cell group movement looks at the FORM as described in this and other passages of Scripture, and tries to create it artificially, hoping that, in doing so, it will produce the LIFE that we read about.

This is what usually happens:
1) The pastor of an institutional church decides, for various reasons, that he wants to convert "his church" into a cell-group church. Alternatively, a "Church planting team" decide that the "church" to be planted will be a house-church.
2) A team of cell group leaders is then chosen from among the congregation. These leaders (sometimes called "servants"), are usually married couples who have a suitable house in which to meet, have been members of the "church" for some time, have a level of maturity, and are in submission to the pastor's leadership. It is important to mention here that all these are good qualities. These leaders (leaders often by name only and not gifting) will then be given some training on how to lead a group. The usual format is that there should be some time of prayer and worship, some time of Bible study, and some time in which people "share together" and perhaps pray for each other. In some cases the "leaders" are given considerable latitude in how they lead, however in most the format and content of the meeting is very tightly controlled by the pastor.

3) Members of the "church" who want to be a part of the small groups are then assigned to a particular group. This may be done in various ways - they may be assigned based on where they live, they may "sign up" for a group of their choice, or the pastor may try to group people together according to personalities, ages, social class, or a host of other considerations.
4) These groups of people, who have been artificially lumped together, are then expected to meet regularly for "fellowship" during which they are to be open and honest with each other, since they are now "friends"! What nonsense! No one can tell you who you are going to be friends with, and any attempt to get you to open up to people that you hardly know or trust is the worst kind of control. This whole concept has more to do with the Freudian ideas of group therapy than with the type of natural and lively relationships we see in real life!
5) If the group stays together, one of two things is likely to happen. The group could stay at a very superficial level, in which everyone pretends that everything is wonderful and that "praise the Lord!" since they have become Christians they have no more problems. Incredible? Does this sound like real life or something that your unsaved family or friends would be excited to be a part of? Alternatively, in response to the heavy expectations, people may feel that, in order to belong, they have no choice but to open up their private lives to others. This can then produce a very unhealthy codependence in the group, and is more akin to the tactics of the cults, than the freedom we are supposed to have in Jesus. In the Kingdom of God we submit to those whom God reveals to us are worthy of our submission, not those who demand it, or threaten us with exclusion if we don't conform. Many people

have subsequently been hurt and betrayed by these types of experiences and, as a result, have become disillusioned with church, and so with God.

From this you will have already, no doubt, pinpointed the flaws in the Cell Group system:

1) It is still an hierarchical structure. The Pastor is still the boss, the cell group leaders report to him, or perhaps to a district leader, who then reports to the pastor. The pastor is still the one who is responsible for the "success" of "his church", and is still the one who controls the whole operation. This is not an escape from Babylon - it is just Babylon rearranged!

As in the institutional church, the Pastor justifies his position by believing that he is responsible before God for the flock under his care. This is the role of the priest in the Old Testament. In the New Testament we are all, individually, priests of the New Covenant (1 Pet 2:9). We are each accountable to God for the choices we make and the actions we take. It is not the pastor's job to make sure that we do not sin. However, as a teacher, every Pastor is subject to a "heavier judgment" (Jas 3:1) since he has assumed the role of leader, he must be very careful that the things he teaches or does do not cause the "least of these who believe in me to stumble" (Matt 18:6). Note, his job is not to prevent them from stumbling, but just not to cause them to stumble. There is thus no justification for the control that the typical pastor or minister exerts over "his" congregation.

2) It is composed of false relationships. Is this how people relate to their families? When they invite their neighbors for a barbecue do they have a designated leader who determines who is going to talk to whom

and what they will talk about? So why do we do that in the "church"? It is simply not being real.

So why do these systems continue? Indeed why have they become so popular?

Over the centuries the concept of "church" has become a package deal with the gospel. On being born again nearly every new believer automatically assumes that now he or she is supposed to "join a church". However, the modern believer who has not been brought up in a traditional church culture has difficulty relating to all the rituals and pageantry, the robes and clerical collars. They are simply too foreign to his life experiences and to his search for meaning and acceptance.

Enter the cell groups. Here is a system that at the same time is both "church" and yet promises to offer deep and meaningful relationships: "Here is a system that will encourage you to grow and develop your spiritual life." And the people seem to be so cheerful and friendly! This is just what the new believer is looking for, and so in he jumps!

Once he is in, it is too late. Perhaps he has never experienced the joy and wonder of deep and honest friendships. In that case he may not even recognize how plastic most of these relationships are. (Please understand, we do recognize that true friendships can and do develop from these relationships - but, to be honest, they are few and far between.)

But if he does realize that the whole set up is superficial and contrived, he will also realize that, if he questions it, he will be told not to be judgmental. To press the issue would be to be cast out and to lose those very relationships that he needs, so he keeps quiet and conforms.

As new believers we are told that the other members of the "church" are our "brothers and sisters in the Lord". This is of course quite correct. However, the assumption that goes along with this is that you will, therefore, spend much time with them. The expectations are often so great that within a year the new believer is so tied up with meetings, prayer groups, Bible studies, Sunday school and other church commitments that he has no time to maintain the relationships he had with friends before he met the Lord. Out goes his sports club membership, his weekly darts game, her sewing or theatre group, and before long he or she has no friends that are not also "church members". How can we be salt and light to our friends and community if we never see them? Instead of remaining as friends, they now become targets for our evangelistic efforts. Our efforts to relate to "the world" become loaded with hidden agendas of getting them converted, in which we include getting them to attend church.

The New Testament describes a body of believers that is characterized by love, service and genuine relationships; a body of people that are so dynamic and positive that they have a tremendous impact on the non-believers around them. The house church movement is a restoration movement that seeks to rediscover and restore these qualities; however they will never succeed in doing so by creating manmade structures and organization.

The movement has tried to create a FORM in the hope that it will produce LIFE.

On your second reading we would suggest that you stop at this point and spend some time praying and meditating about the things you have read and how they apply to you. The following questions may help you in this process:

Read through the first five chapters of Acts and ask yourself the following questions:
1) Is the life that you read about in this passage being generated by life or form?

2) Why has the cell-group movement experienced such growth and what does that tell you?

3) If you were to experience some type of personal tragedy, who would you confide in and why?

4) Does the man in the street relate to, and confide in, his friends because someone else has defined for him those he should relate to, or because of a bonding that life itself creates?

Chapter 7

HOW DID WE ARRIVE HERE?

Change and traditions are inevitable

When the Church started it was a loose, informal gathering of all those people who had personally known and followed Jesus. Before too long, Pentecost had swelled the numbers, but the structure of the group continued to be very simple - the disciples would meet daily in the temple courts and in their homes (Acts 2:46). At that time the Church consisted entirely of Jews and Gentiles from other nations who had converted to Judaism (Acts 2:5). They had much in common, particularly the legacies of the Old Testament customs.

Over the next 2000 years however, the Church would have to endure both times of persecution and of favor. It would have to deal with numerous heresies, and would have to adapt to countless different customs. Leaders, all imperfect and sinful, would rise and fall. Throughout all of this the Church would have to work out, in real life, "what are the essentials of the Christian faith?", "Who is, and who is not a Christian, (those going around doing the works of Christ)?" "What practices and traditions are to remain unchanged, and which can be modified to suit local conditions?" "How is the

Church to relate to the secular government, both in times of opposition, and in times of favor?".

The answers to these questions are not spelled out in Scripture. Indeed, the Church first had to decide what was and what was not to be accepted as Scripture. All of this was, and is, no easy task. Therefore it is hardly a surprise, indeed it is to be expected, that over the ages the Church would change. Some of these changes are good, some bad. Behind all of them there is a story and an intense, unseen, spiritual conflict.

As we look at the Church today, with all its divisions, controversies, and problems, we are faced with the same questions - what do we keep, what do we throw out? In order to answer these, we must understand the changes that the Church has gone through, what the traditions mean, and for what reason they arose.

This then is our task. We do not intend to examine in detail every event of Church history, for we are not Church historians. But we do seek to discover the trends and significant events that have dramatically changed the way the Church has operated.

Are all traditions bad?

Human beings, by nature, are creatures of habit. We like structure. We like to know how we are supposed to do things, and what is going to happen next. All of us have numerous traditions by which we live. Without them life would be total chaos, as each morning we would wake up and have to decide whether today we would get dressed before eating, or eat before dressing. And what should we wear today? A grass skirt? A fancy western suit? An army uniform? The customs and traditions of our society mean that we do not have to think about these things in detail every single day.

Traditions in themselves are not necessarily bad. This applies also to the church. But in evaluating them, we need to ask some questions.

Are they biblical?

Some traditions, such as baptism, and the Lord's supper are clearly Scriptural. Others, such as the distinction between clergy and laity, are clearly contrary to Scripture. Most, however, will be neither.

Are they helpful?

Do the customs draw us closer to God and to our fellow men? Do they help or hinder us in growing in faith and obedience?

The distinction between Form and Function

In many cases different churches will have different ways of performing the same function. Every church, for example, has a different tradition regarding baptism, how it is performed and what words are said by whom. Clearly the function of baptism is important and Scriptural, but is the form, the manner in which it is performed, also important? While the Scriptures do not, for example, give any clear detailed directions about the Lord's Supper, the form used by the Corinthian church had clearly become unacceptable and needed to be reformed (1 Cor 11:17-34).

The factors behind the traditions

Before we look at some of the specific events of Church history, we need to identify some of the factors that have been behind the developments:

The effects of heresy

The rise of specific heresies has been one of the main factors that has prompted the Church to define itself more precisely. It is in response to these that we have discovered such important concepts as the *Trinity*. It is also the main reason why we have developed creeds and other formulations of just what it is that we believe.

At the same time, in order to try to protect us from any possible deviation from truth, we have, like the Pharisees, hemmed ourselves in with countless rules and rituals. It is here that we find the root of the various liturgies that would pre-define every word the leader and congregation are to say when they meet together in worship; a far cry from the informality of the early church.

So we need to find a Spirit led balance. How do we provide freedom for people to be spontaneous, and to ask questions so that they can grow, to disagree with the leaders, while still providing sufficient guidelines so that people can live in harmony?

The effects of culture

In the early church, children were circumcised, no one ate pork, and they went into the Jewish temple to worship. Would the Gentile churches have to do the same? As the faith has spread from one people to another, these basic questions have to be asked again. The culture in which the Church grows will inevitably influence their styles of worship, use of music, dress codes etc. Some of these changes have become traditions that are as strong as that of not eating pork, and have been forced upon peoples to whom the traditions are totally alien.

At times we have also seen pagan ideas and superstitions enter the church. Some have been modified, such as the development of Christmas from a pagan festival to the "birthday" of Jesus; others have led the Church astray, such as the development of "indulgences" to buy a deceased relative out of purgatory. (The concept of an indulgence was that a relative could buy ceremonial articles from the church that would release the dead relative from purgatory and into heaven. The price of the indulgence was often so high that the living relatives were plunged into poverty by their desperate attempt to buy a better future for their departed loved ones.)

The effects of politics

The interaction between Church and state has always been an uneasy one. In times of persecution the Church has behaved in certain ways. In times of peace, it has had different challenges with which to deal.

The structure of civil authority also had its impact, and to a large extent determined the organization of church leadership and government.

The effects of human nature

Church leadership has certainly not been immune from the problems caused by internal politics, power struggles, greed, corruption, and other manifestations of human sinfulness.

The effects of ignorance and confusion

At times, simply not knowing the truth has resulted in wrong decisions being taken, which have then become enshrined in immutable and unquestioned tradition. For example, confusion about the distinction between the modalities and the sodalities (discussed in detail below) of the Church have seriously hampered the missionary expansion of the gospel.

Let us now look at what happened historically. Just what was the original Church like, and how did it become what it is today?

WHAT WAS THE CHURCH LIKE IN THE BEGINNING?

When and where they met

In Acts we see the Church meeting mostly in homes. There were no church buildings until the third or fourth century when the church was allowed to own property in its own name (see David Barrett's *World Christian Movement*). The believers in each locality had their own leaders. There was no organizational structure above the local fellowship of believers. The believers in one locality related to the believers of other areas on the basis of friendship and brotherhood by virtue of their shared loyalty to the person and teaching of Jesus Christ.

Since the meetings consisted of relatively small numbers, they were able to operate in a participative and informal manner in which every member would have opportunity to participate with a "hymn, or word of instruction...", each person, hopefully, giving due respect to others who might want to speak (1 Cor 14:26-33).

This meeting, and especially the communal meal, were considered so important that believers would readily risk their lives to meet in secret together. Furthermore, portions of the bread and wine would be taken back to those who were unable to attend because of sickness or imprisonment.

Baptism and Lord's Supper

At first, both of these rites were very simple. New believers were quickly baptized on the basis of a simple confession of faith that "Jesus is Lord". Initially baptism was by immersion, preferably in "living water" (e.g. a river or stream), but, by as early as the end of the first century, baptism by sprinkling or pouring was the most common means. Still, however, the use of living water was the preferred method. The triadic formula of baptism into the "name of the Father, and of the Son, and of the Holy Spirit" was not developed until the 2nd century.

As stated above, the Lord's Supper was celebrated weekly as a very special and sacred event. All those who were not yet baptized believers were excluded, and it was also considered a severe punishment to be excluded from the meal because of church discipline.

Leadership

During the first 30 to 50 years of the early church, leaders were recognized solely by virtue of their innate leadership qualities, and the evidence of the gifts (conforming to the ministry gifts of apostle, prophet, evangelist, pastor and teacher, as identified Eph 4:11 and 1 Cor 12:29). It seems clear that these leaders had spiritual authority (cf. 1 Thess 5:12) that stems, not from their appointment to an office, but rather from their anointing by God, in much the same way that Paul had authority in the churches because he was an apostle "called by the will of God" (1 Cor 1:1). This seems particularly evident from Paul's letters to the Corinthians in which he identifies that they were having problems about whose ministry (e.g. Paul's or Apollos'), or what form of ministry, was the most important. In answer, Paul stresses that each person should function according to the gifts placed in them, implying that each one has importance and authority within the realm of that gifting.

Paul himself took a very active role in providing input and oversight to the churches - even to those that he had not founded himself (such as the Church in Rome). His only claim to such authority was his personal calling and commissioning as an apostle and the confirmation of that authority and calling was that the churches listened to him! James also stressed the tremendous responsibility carried by leaders, warning people not to presume to be teachers unless clearly called by the Spirit (James 3:1). The implication is that already people were aspiring to positions of leadership.

As a closely knit body of believers, the early churches looked after their own affairs. Indeed the fact that the disciples were so close knit and self reliant was one of the main reasons that they were perceived as a threat to the local government and unbelieving people. The local churches would settle their own conflicts, try their own disputes, and enforce their own standards of behavior without any reference to the Roman courts of law. In 1 Cor 6 we see that Paul was exasperated by one group of believers who were not doing this.

The standards of behavior expected were very high and any breach resulted in dis-fellowship according to Matt 18:17. Initially it seems that, once dis-fellowshipped, it was extremely difficult to be restored, and this became the subject of much debate over the next couple of centuries.

Ministry to the poor

At the Council of Jerusalem (Acts 15) the apostles, including Paul (Gal 2:10) agreed that the Gentile believers might have freedom from the Law of the Jews, but that they must continue to "remember the poor". This instruction was clearly followed with great diligence for the early disciples were noted for their remarkable generosity. At that time, of course, the Church, of itself, owned no property, so any alms given to the Church were immediately distributed amongst those who had need (see for example Acts 4:34-35).

The Development of Customs, Traditions, and Rules

While the apostles and other first-hand witnesses of Jesus were still alive, and while the Church was still small, it was perhaps relatively easy to resolve disputes and controversies about doctrine and the conduct of the church - one simply appealed to the nearest apostle for clarification or a decision. As the apostles died off, however, these questions became much more critical. What was the truth? How could we know? How was the Church to operate?

These questions were urgently debated, and largely resolved, during the period from the end of the first century through to the fourth. At the same time, the Church had already developed some customs and traditions, the very presence of which provided some sense of unity and identity to the widely scattered congregations.

THE CLERGY AND LAITY

Bishops, Presbyters, and Deacons

As the churches grew, and as their weekly assemblies grew in size, they could no longer function as informal gatherings with a "participatory" or "democratic" style of leadership. Increasingly it became necessary, and natural, for meetings to be more structured, with one or more leaders providing firm direction and guidance. By the end of the first century most churches had a fairly established hierarchy with a bishop and elders being in charge, and a number of deacons (*diakoneo* "servant, one who ministers to another's needs") who were seen as the elders' assistants.

In some churches the bishop was over the rest of the elders; in others he was merely the chairman amongst his colleagues. The bishop was elected by the congregation, and during the second century it became the custom for neighboring bishops to come and lay hands on the candidate to install him into office. Once in office, he had responsibility for the administrative supervision of the church, including the appointment of the elders and deacons.

As concern for the purity of rites such as baptism and the Lord's supper developed, the privilege of presiding over the rite was confined to the bishop, and (but only in his absence) to the elders. Since he offered the prayers and the liturgy of the Eucharist, he also became known as "priest" (*sacerdos* or *hiereus*)

This development was supported by the following factors:
1) Increased size of congregations
2) The move from "face-to-face" meetings to "front-led" meetings.

Natural leadership
Naturally, among a group of elders there would be one who would usually provide leadership to the group. When a new elder was to be added, it would be natural for the bishop to preside at the ordination ceremony. With time, this courtesy became an exclusive right.

Correspondence between churches
As churches sent representatives to each other, it would often be the bishop that was sent, thus enhancing his status as the leader, particularly if the occasion of his visit was to lay hands on and ordain a new minister in another church.

Illiteracy
Without a doubt, illiteracy is a prominent reason for the development of the priestly orders and hierarchical structures. If people cannot read, they are dependant on the leader to read the Scriptures for them. This enhances the status of those who can read (and thus can for themselves study and understand God's word) as compared to those who are illiterate and ignorant.

This was further compounded by the development of the idea that the Scriptures were simply too deep to be understood by the ordinary person, and that only a trained priest could rightly read and interpret them. Knowledge is power, and those with such power did not want to lose it!

The claims of apostolic succession

As the Gnostic heresy developed, people increasingly looked for "one voice of authority" to decide on matters of truth and doctrine.

As people looked for evidence to back their denunciation of Gnosticism, they searched for the teachings and traditions of Jesus and the original apostles. But who could reliably attest to such traditions? The defense put forward by the churches was that the apostles had handed down the truths to their successors in leadership. Thus the present bishop, being the direct successor of an apostle, was the guardian of the truth and thus the final authority against the claims of Gnosticism.

Synods and Regional Councils

As various heresies surfaced, the churches would gather together the bishops of the prominent churches as a synod or council in order to come to a resolution of the matter, much as the Church did at the first council of Jerusalem.

Patriarchal churches and Popes

The churches in the largest cities (Rome, Alexandria, Carthage, Antioch) gradually grew in influence. This was because of their size, and also because, being located in cosmopolitan cities, they were affected by developments occurring in every region of Christendom, and so also had an opinion on all these developments.

Also, as city congregations grew, they planted daughter churches in the suburbs of the cities. Often these would be led by an elder who would remain under the authority of the mother church's bishop (instead of releasing the churches to be fully independent and equal). The influence of the largest churches extended even further, becoming a "father" influence over whole regions. The bishops of these churches came to be known as "papas" or "popes". Rome, being at the capital and cross-roads of the Roman empire, naturally became the most prominent. This was further boosted by their claim to apostolic succession from Peter and Paul.

In time, of course, the western Roman Catholic Church claimed infallibility for its Pope, based on this same line of succession.

LITURGY AND RITES

Baptismal Creeds

From the beginning, both baptism and the Lord's Supper were considered as cornerstones of the life of the Church. At the very first, as in Philip's baptism of the Ethiopian (Acts 8:36-38), it was a fairly informal rite, done immediately after conversion (see also Acts 16:31-33). Before long, however, it became much more solemnized. Probably by the end of the first century the baptism was being done only by the bishop or elder or, in their absence, a deacon. The proceedings would usually start with some form of declaration of belief. According to Tertullian (AD 200) and implied by Acts 8:37 (found in only some manuscripts), this was often done by asking the candidate if he believed in Jesus Christ, to which he would respond "I believe". This would be followed by a renunciation of the devil accompanied, at times, by exorcism. The candidate would then be baptized by immersion, or more commonly, by pouring, after which he would be anointed with oil and hands were laid on him with prayer for the gift of the Holy Spirit.

In the second century the triadic "Father, Son and Holy Spirit" was the common formula but, as heresies arose and people wanted to be more precise as to what they did or did not believe, the creeds were developed.

Since baptism was particularly associated with the concept of resurrection, it came also to be associated with Easter. With time, this became the only time at which it was held, and it became the practice to teach the candidates (or "catechumens") during the period of Lent, leading up to Easter.

Eucharistic formulations

This same process was seen with the Lord's Supper. Initially it was simply a meal in which believers would join together to "give thanks" (eucharistia). Gradually it evolved into a complex and highly structured liturgy. Between the third and fourth century the idea that the bread and wine were supernaturally transformed into the Lord's body and blood developed.

Church Discipline

Through repentance and baptism, believers could receive forgiveness of sin and enter into new life with Jesus. But what about those that sinned after baptism? Could the Church permit sinners to remain in fellowship? Hebrews, for example, states that "if we deliberately sin after receiving the knowledge of the truth there no longer remains a sacrifice for sins." (Heb 10:26). And 1 Cor 6 & Rev 21 both make it clear that idolaters, adulterers, etc will have no place in Heaven, and Paul exhorts the Corinthians to "expel the wicked man from among you." (1 Cor 5:13). Furthermore, 1 John 5:16 also seems to indicate that there are some sins for which there is no forgiveness, though for lesser sins restoration was possible. Initially, then, Church discipline seems to have been very strict, with very high standards. Those that fell from grace were out, with no second chance. The Church was seen as the "assembly of the righteous" and membership in it as the "ark" to salvation (in reference to Noah's ark of salvation). By the opening of the third century, there were three categories of sin:1. **Minor sin**, which was dealt with by open confession, mutual forgiveness, prayer, fasting and almsgiving.

2. **Grave sin**, which could be dealt with by a long period of penitence, which had to be formally approved by the church. This was granted as a one-time-only "second chance"; any further sin could not be forgiven.

3. **Mortal sin**, which could under no circumstances be forgiven, and which led to automatic excommunication from the church.

At this same time, however, there was a growing move to allow the forgiveness (after penitence) of grave and even mortal sins. Callistus (217-222) of Rome based this authority on the Lord's command to let the wheat and the weeds "grow together until the harvest" (Matt 13:29-30).

This perspective was strengthened during the coming persecutions of AD 250. At this time multitudes of Christians escaped death by buying false certificates proving that they had worshipped the Roman gods. These weak Christians then sought readmission to the church on the basis that it was their courage, and not their faith, that had failed. They were supported in this by those who had been imprisoned and tortured and who felt their virtue gave them the authority to pardon their weaker brothers. Even those who had actually sacrificed to the gods were pardoned, although often only on their death beds.

Thus in time the view of Callistus prevailed. The church became not just the society of the redeemed, but a hospital in which sinners could be brought to salvation. All sins were forgivable after suitable confession and penance, and even the doctrine of unforgivable sin lapsed.

Sodalities and Modalities

From the beginning, the Church has always existed in two phases, the geographically stationary "local" Church, and the mobile "apostolic wing". While Paul was initially a part of the Church in Antioch, and indeed was commissioned and sent out from there, it is clear that his ministry was more than just being an arm of his Antioch church. Indeed, through his travels he planted new churches, and brought oversight, teaching, and disciplinary correction to established churches. Acting merely as a representative of the local Church in Antioch, he would have no such right. Clearly he and his apostolic team had become a separate, independent, although still interdependent wing of the universal Church. The implication is that Apollos operated in the same manner.

In technical terms the trans-local missionary band is called a sodality, while the Church that is resident in a particular locality is a modality. The sodality, by nature, always consists of those who have received a call to take the gospel further a field than their local community. Although frequently misunderstood by Christians, the sodalities have always existed. Indeed, they have been the main means by which the Church has expanded into new territory. They have also frequently been the means by which the local Christian community has been encouraged, rebuked, and brought back into greater purity and holiness.

In the first century it was the apostles and their teams; in later centuries it was the monks and nuns. At times these structures also fell into corruption, but at other times they carried the torch far and wide (consider, for example, Augustine, St. Francis of Assisi).

Divisions and Dissensions

Division and church splits are neither new nor just a phenomenon of the Protestant Movement. Indeed, while all the time declaring that the Church is "one body", Church history has been marked by divisions. The early division of the Church into three - the Roman, the Orthodox Eastern, and the Coptic (African), has had a major impact on world history, even though all three largely kept the same hierarchy with a single Pope at the head.

While most of the splits hinged on a disagreement about a doctrine, they were also largely fuelled by personality and other issues. The conflict over Easter serves as one such example:

Easter

Jesus ate His Passover meal with His disciples on the evening of the 14th day of Nisan, was crucified the following day, and rose three days later, early on the first day of the week (Sunday).

The practice of the Church in Asia Minor was to celebrate Easter with a vigil that ended with a Eucharistic meal on the evening of the 14th day of Nisan, whatever day of the week that might be. Roman custom, however, was to celebrate the Eucharist on the Sunday following Passover.

In AD 154 or 155 Polycarp of Smyrna visited Anicetus, Bishop of Rome, to try to resolve this difference. They could not, but parted amicably, agreeing to differ.

By AD 190 the situation had become so divisive, especially in the Roman church where they had individuals coming from both traditions that, in the following years, Victor, Bishop of Rome, contrived several synods at which he decreed in favor of the Roman tradition. Asia Minor refused to conform and so Victor promptly excommunicated them all!

The Reformation

By the time of Luther in the 16th century, the Roman church was in a serious state. Corruption and immorality in the hierarchy, veneration of the saints and of Mary, the sale of indulgences and pilgrimages for the dead, collections of relics and burning of witches abounded. Once more it was time for God to act.

Back to the Word, but what about Love?

The major victory of the reformation was of course to re-establish the primary importance of the Scriptures, the doctrine of salvation by grace, not works, and the priesthood of all believers. But, to a large extent these victories were in theory rather than in practice. Luther had restored the original theological foundations for the Church, but it has been left, and continues to be left, to those that follow after him to rebuild the building on this foundation. Since that time, there has been wave after wave of different "reformations" in which one group or another have identified another aspect of the Scriptures that needed to be restored. So, for example, the Anabaptists restored the "Believers Baptism", and John Calvin returned to the congregation a voice in the appointing of church leaders. He also restored the churches' right to discipline wayward members, up to the point of excommunication.

Future reformers have returned more truth to the Church. But with each development, a split has occurred; some have believed and moved on with the new truth, some have held on firmly to the old tradition. In many cases the conflicts have not been about absolute issues of right or wrong, but rather arguments (like the Easter controversy) about traditions and customs. And often these conflicts have been bitter and hurtful, bringing deep divisions into the body of Christ.

The loss of the sodality

When the Protestant church split away from the Roman church, it concentrated almost exclusively on the development of the local church congregation. The whole concept of the sodality was lost, and the result was an almost total lack of any Protestant missionary activity for 200 years.

In 1792 William Carey published *An Enquiry into the Obligation of Christians to Use Means for the Conversion of the Heathens*. It provoked an outburst of controversy, but through it the Protestant Church rediscovered the sodality, now in the form of a mission agency. From that time the missionary movement has multiplied, but still, it seems, the local churches do not understand it. Usually what has happened is that a team of believers would be sent out by a local Christian community as missionaries to a foreign land.

At this point, like the early Roman church, the sending church would attempt to rein in both the missionaries and the new churches to make them conform and submit to the paternal authority of the sending church (now called a "denomination"). Almost without exception, where this has happened it has led to the clipping of the wings of the missionary band, and to the establishment in the newly planted churches of traditions that are barely relevant in the sending church, never-mind in the culture and society of the new churches.

Furthermore, not even fully understanding the concept of the sodality themselves, the missionaries have planted local churches, and have failed to pass on the concept of sodality and the need for the new churches to be involved in cross-cultural missions themselves.

WHAT DOES THIS ALL MEAN TO US TODAY?

Are we to simply accept the traditions of the church in which we have been raised and nurtured? Or are we to examine all matters of faith and conduct in order to conform ourselves to God's ideal?

We believe that we must, like the Bereans (Acts 17:11), examine all things to see if they are in line with Scripture, and this includes the practices and traditions of our churches. However, there are several principles to which we must hold fast:

The Supremacy of Love (1 Cor 13)

In seeking after truth we can only look to our own lives. We cannot, and dare not, condemn our brothers, for in the end they will be answerable to the Lord, not to us, for all they have said and done. And so will we. Let us be sure that we do not fall short on love.

Let us therefore be very patient with our brothers and sisters who do not seem to have the same degree of revelation or understanding that we think we do, "for if you think you are standing firm, be careful that you don't fall!" (1 Cor 10:12). Our purpose is for the Church to grow in maturity, and so in unity, not for yet more divisions and arguments!

The Supremacy of Values and Principles over and above Practices

We must know what we believe as Biblical absolutes, and we must know what are not absolutes. On the basis of these values, we must define the principles by which we shall live, principles such as integrity and honesty, patience and love, worship and giving to the poor.

Only then, after we have defined our foundations, can we start to develop or examine our traditions and practices, for once we place more value on the way we do things, than on the reason why we do them, we are in deep trouble.

What do we learn from History?

Through all the different events of history, one theme seems to stand out: in seeking to be doctrinally correct, we have exchanged the warm, informal, but radical, fellowship of the early believers for structured, hierarchical organizations that are hamstrung by their rules, regulations, traditions and customs. In the words of Jesus we "strain out a gnat but swallow a camel." (Matt 23:24).

Given what we know about human nature, this is hardly a surprising development. But God wants more for his children, for "it is for freedom that Christ has set us free" (Gal 5:1).

A few more titbits (quoted from The Open Church by James Rutz)

"What's so special about 11 AM?

Martin Luther faithfully preached every Sunday at dawn. The hour was exactly the same that the Catholic mass had been scheduled for aeons. Luther, however, did not enjoy getting up early. (Night owls, take comfort!) What he really preferred was to go down to the tavern or sit in his kitchen and talk theology with his friends and drink beer on Saturday night. In fact, the tune of his famous hymn, "A Mighty Fortress Is Our God," was a popular German drinking song of his day.

So, before long, he moved the Protestant worship service to the saner hour of 9 AM-though not without sustaining numerous complaints from the early bird faction.

But the older he got, the longer he talked on Saturday night and the more beer he drank! He moved the service to 10 AM. to the tune of more complaints. But still as he talked longer, he found that even 10 AM to be uncomfortably early. The last possible hour he could set for the service and still call it Morning Worship was 11.00 AM. So he did. And that is how it came about that 500,000,000 Protestants today hold church services every Sunday at 11.00 AM!

And Speaking of Clothes...

The clerical "backwards collar" deserves to be awarded a small note here. At one brief point in European history, every man who could afford a suit had a shirt or two with a reverse collar. It was simply the style du jour. Eventually, however, it went the way of all styles, and no one wore it any more except, that is, for the clergy. Being perpetually underpaid, ministers and missionaries have not been noted for up to the minute fashions. And, in this particular case, they continued to wear the now venerable collar simply because they didn't have the money to refurbish their wardrobes with newer suits."

On your second reading we would suggest that you stop at this point and spend some time praying and meditating about the things you have read and how they apply to you. The following questions may help you in this process:

1) Please identify all the Scriptures which indicate that the pastor is head of the local church. (See how many you can find)!
2) Ask to see the budget of the "church" that you are part of, and see if you can discover what percentage of the gross income goes to directly helping the poor, in relationship to that which is spent on salaries and buildings. Peter's request to Paul was to remember the poor. Do you think that Peter would be happy with how your church spends its money?

Chapter 8

THE CHURCH OF THE KINGDOM

"I saw the Holy City, the new Jerusalem, coming down out of heaven from God, prepared as a bride beautifully dressed for her husband." (Rev 21:2)

The New Jerusalem symbolically represents the perfected Bride of Christ (i.e. the true Church, all those who are true believers in Jesus.) At the same time, it also represents the rule of God, a society in which "I shall be their God and they shall be My people." (Jer 31:33; Rev 21:3) and in which every believer reigns as a king (Rev 2:26-27; 3:21; 22:5). Jesus said "I will build my Church" (Matt 16:18), but what is His Church? What is its purpose? How does it fulfill that purpose and what prevents it from being all that it should be?

Ekklesia - a called out people

"To the Church (*ekklesia*) of God at Corinth" (1 Cor 1:2).

"the Church (*ekklesia*) which meets at his [Nymphas'] house" (Col 4:15).

"[they] gathered the Church (*ekklesia*) together" (Acts 14:27).

Throughout the New Testament, the Greek word used for "Church" is *ecclesia*, from which we get words such as "ecclesiastic". Its original meaning was "a group of people who have been called out of their homes into a public assembly". When used in various parts of Scripture it refers sometimes to a local assembly of believers who met together in a particular place, and at other times to the world-wide, universal assembly of believers. At no time does it refer to a building - the Church in those days did not even own a "church building". Of course most Christians would agree with this, and yet at the same time they will continue to talk about "going to church" or "the church on the street corner". It is out of the fullness of the heart that the mouth speaks, and such talk clearly indicates that in their hearts they do not understand this concept.

"And the Lord added to their number [ecclesia] daily those that were being saved" (Acts 2:47).

"And He is the head of the body, the Church" (Col 1:18) - The Church is the body of Christ, i.e. all believers.

Scripture is very clear that it is the people who are the Church since we have all been called out of the dominion of darkness and into the family of God, being made His children (John 1). We ourselves have become "the Temple of the living God" (2 Cor 6:16), both individually and collectively as the Church, for it is in us that God Himself chooses to live!

> "As God has said: 'I will live with them and walk among them, and I will be their God and they will be my people" (2 Cor 6:16).

> "I have been crucified with Christ and I no longer live, but CHRIST LIVES IN ME." (Gal 2:20). "You also, like living stones, are being built into a spiritual house to be a holy priesthood, offering spiritual sacrifices acceptable to God through Jesus Christ." (2 Pet 2:5).

Once we understand that God has made His home IN US, then we, the Church, become His dwelling place. It is meaningless to talk of "going to church" for how can we go to church when we are the church? It is meaningless also to talk about going to "the house of the Lord" in order to worship Him.

In the days of the Old Covenant, God was to be worshipped in the Temple, which was indeed His dwelling place, and which was filled with His glory. When the first Temple was dedicated to God by Solomon we read that:

> "Fire came down from heaven and consumed the burnt offering and the sacrifices, and the glory of the LORD filled the temple. The priests could not enter the temple of the LORD because the glory of the LORD filled it." 2 Chr 7:1-2

So powerful was God's presence that the High Priest was permitted into the Holy of Holies only once a year, and then only after elaborate sacrifices had been made.

But now God has made a NEW COVENANT in which this same glory now LIVES IN US. Worship does indeed take place in the Temple, but now the Temple is our own bodies and, by the grace of God, the Holy of Holies is now our very own hearts!

"A time is coming when you will worship the Father neither on this mountain nor in Jerusalem [i.e. in the temple]...Yet a time is coming and has now come when the true worshippers will worship the Father in spirit and in truth, for they are the kind of worshippers the Father seeks. God is spirit, and His worshippers must worship in spirit and in truth." (John 4:21-24).

Since God lives in us, our worship occurs not in buildings but inside us, in our spirits as our spirits commune daily and constantly with God's Spirit. We cannot "go to church" to worship for we are the Church, and worship occurs wherever we are - in our homes, on the streets, in bed, even in the bathroom! This also means that a Church meeting occurs whenever and wherever the Church meets (not just on Sundays).

"For where two or three come together in My name, there am I with them." (Matt 18:20).

The early Church was just that - an early (immature) Church

In the early chapters of Acts we see the dramatic growth of the early Church. At that time it seems that the Church was full of freedom and life, with the disciples eager to learn from the apostles, and eager to share their possessions with the poor and needy. We also see that "a large number of priests became obedient to the faith" (Acts 6:7). Unfortunately it is also clear that many of these priests and the Jewish believers brought with them many of the traditions and customs of the Old Covenant. Not only did they still expect everyone to be circumcised (Acts 15:5), but they were also still making sacrifices at the Temple.

> "Then they [James and the elders at Jerusalem] said to Paul: *'You see brother, how many thousands of Jews have believed, and all of them are zealous for the law."* (Acts 21:20).

So strong was their allegiance to the Law, that they even required Paul to make an offering at the temple (v26). The unbelieving Jews put up with the Jerusalem Church because, despite being Christians, they still followed all the requirements of the Law, and so did not offend the Jews. But when Paul came he preached against the Law, saying that it was useless and designed only for lawbreakers, since the only way to God was through grace and faith. This thoroughly upset the unbelieving Jews, who then plotted to kill him (Acts 23). This strong allegiance to the Temple by the early Church is undoubtedly the reason why God had the Romans destroy the temple in AD 70.

Similarly, as we look through the letters to the Corinthians, Galatians, Ephesians, Colossians etc. we find in each one that major corrections were needed as the early Church had not fully understood the freedoms, and the responsibilities, of the New Covenant. Few churches today, for example, would put up with the drunken revelry or sexual immorality in which the Corinthians engaged (1 Cor 5 & 11). In almost all the letters, the major emphasis is that in Christ we are free. Clearly the churches then had not fully grasped this, and unfortunately churches today are no closer to doing so.

We cannot therefore hold up the early Church as a model that we must strive to copy. On the contrary, we must base our concept of Church on Christ's teaching, using the successes and failures of the early Church as teaching examples for us.

ON THIS BASIS WHAT IS THE CHURCH CALLED TO BE A DO?

On your second reading we would suggest that you stop at this point and spend some time praying and meditating about the things you have read and how they apply to you. The following questions may help you in this process:

1) Where did Jesus spend most of His time when he was on Earth? Was it:

a) In meetings at the Synagogue?
b) With those He had chosen to disciple?
c) In taverns and bars with sinners and tax collectors?
d) In prayer by Himself?

When He was engaged in b, c, or d, above, was He any less engaged in being Christ than when He was in the religious meetings?

When we, as the body of Christ, are engaged in b, c or d, are we any less engaged in being the Church than when we are in a religious meeting?

In which setting do you think He was most productive in advancing the Kingdom of God?

2) What is the minimum number of people needed in order to have a Church meeting (i.e. a meeting of the Church)? Does the Bible indicate that this meeting has to take place on any particular day or in any particular place? Is there any location in which such a meeting can not be called Church? Justify your answers with reference to Scripture.

3) Where do you spend most of your time and energies?
4) Do the activities through which you express your faith more closely resemble the priorities of Jesus, or are they determined by the traditions and expectations of your church?
5) In response to your answers to these questions, and in accordance with the priorities that Jesus demonstrated, what changes do you need to make with regard to how you use your time and where you expend your energies?

Chapter 9

CHURCH DEFINED BY LOVE NOT STRUCTURE

As one looks at the original Church in Jerusalem it is clear that, right from the beginning of this new movement, Satan had a clear plan to divert the attention of those in authority away from the Word of God (which is Jesus) to the administrative issues that were arising due to the number of people that had been added. However the Apostles were adamant in their response, stating, "It would not be right for us to neglect the Word of God and wait on tables" (Acts 6:2). What we do see happen is the disciples, right at the beginning of their roles within the Church, giving away responsibility. It seems that the Apostles were not interested in who had control, but more interested in obeying the commands of Christ. As a footnote, it is also interesting to note that it was not the Apostles who appointed the administrators, they were happy to allow the people to work it out for themselves.

If we were to plot this on an organizational chart it would look something like this.

JESUS
Believers Believers Believers Believers Believers
(each individually accountable to Christ, each encouraging each other to stand firm)

Leaders and Elders
(each intent on serving and helping the believers to obey Christ - Eph 4:12)

First of all, Jesus is the Head of the Church (Eph 5:23). Then, since each one of us is a priest (1 Peter 2:9) with direct personal access to "the Boss" (Heb 4:16) there is no hierarchy between us and Jesus. Finally, since to be a leader is to be a servant or a slave (Mark 10:43-44), on an organizational chart they will be placed below us as they do all they can to lift us up to greater holiness and obedience to Christ.

How is this worked out on the ground, in the context of the Church in a particular locality? To be able to examine this, we have to discard all our previously held notions of what "Church" should look like. Since every culture, and every city, town and village is different, it is impossible to lay down any rules about how a local group of believers should be organized. Indeed, since the essence of the Kingdom of God is life rather than rigid structure, we cannot prescribe the "right way" to do it. That could become a legalistic framework in itself! In fact, it will be clear from the previous discussion that we do not even need to think about how the Church should be structured, as we are not the ones who are supposed to structure it! Whoever we are (or think we are) our job is simply to personally OBEY CHRIST and to MAKE DISCIPLES and to let God do the rest. To this end, the following guidelines may be helpful:

1) No individual, or group of individuals, is to decide how the Church should be organized, or how and

when the Church should meet. The nature of Church is that it is the informal gathering of believers in whatever arrangements provide the most life for them: two or three might regularly meet in a home to pray and study together; a dozen may meet daily with an anointed teacher; a couple might seek out an older, mature Christian with pastoral gifts (an "elder") for help with their marriage. At times (but not on a rigid schedule) the Church may congregate in larger numbers to hear from a visiting apostle, to read a letter from a missionary, or to attend a conference or retreat.

2) There is no Biblical account whatsoever of professional leaders in the New Testament, let alone any who received a salary - after all, it is no-one's job to "run the Church". This model of Church government is not rooted in the New Testament and has been mightily used by Satan to divide up the body of Christ into professionals and amateurs - the clergy and laity.

That does not, however, preclude individuals from providing individual financial support for any Christian leader (or otherwise) that they might chose. Offerings may be taken up for specific projects or ministries, but should probably not be routinely collected for the "routine" running of the Church. In fact, since there are no officials and no building there should be almost no regular expenses! This means that almost all the money that individuals donate can go directly to ministries that affect the poor, the oppressed, and the unreached!

3) There should be no structured procedure for becoming a "member" of the Church i.e. no "new member's course", confirmation or catechism classes - every

true believer, once he or she has confessed Jesus as Lord, AUTOMATICALLY becomes a member of the Church. Therefore any lists that you may have are not membership lists, but merely the names and addresses of other brothers and sisters in the Lord that you know. It is important to add, at this point, that we recognize and fully support the many support groups that are started for new believers. It is of vital importance that each of us is fully rooted and grounded in the faith. However this group should be for instruction, fellowship and encouragement not membership!

4) Baptisms of believers may be performed by ANY true believer, although younger Christians may be wise to seek counsel from an elder before performing a baptism. Those believers who earnestly seek baptism should not be refused, nor should they be told to wait (see how quickly the Ethiopian was baptized in Acts 8:36).

5) There is only one Church, therefore those that meet regularly together (e.g. for a fellowship meal) should not give themselves a name. Names are very powerful, and end up producing a concept of ownership (i.e. a sense of us as separate from them, our members as distinct from their members), and with it pride, jealousy and competition - remember the tower of Babel! In Revelation Jesus names the individual Churches by town or location.

6) Jesus said "do this in remembrance of me" (Luke 22:19). As believers we should frequently remember the Lord's death by sharing together in the bread and wine, perhaps every time that we eat a meal together. Note that ANY believer can initiate this. It is not a ritual that requires the presence of an "ordained minister or priest" since every one of us is a minister and a priest (1 Peter 2:9). The Scriptures give no

indication whatsoever that communion should be taken at a particular time or place, or in any particular manner.

What about Elders and Deacons?

In the New Testament it is quite clear that Paul appointed elders in various towns, and also that he instructed others, like Titus, to also appoint elders and deacons (Acts 14:23; Tit 1:5). However, it is interesting to note that these two Scriptures are the only references to the appointment of elders, and even then there is no indication of the method by which they were appointed (e.g., by voting, casting lots, etc). In his letter to Timothy, Paul lays out the character requirements for those who should be overseers and helpers in the assembly, but gives no instructions on how to appoint them to the job. In the other Scriptural references the elders simply seem to be there, with no indication of how they got there, other than the fact that they "were reputed to be pillars" (Gal 2:9). In 1 Pet 5:1 Peter uses the term "elder" but then in verse 5 he speaks to the "younger" people. One can only conclude that he is using the term not as a job title, but simply as a description for those who have advanced in the Christian life through many years of experience. One wonders how often the word is used in this sense in the other Scriptures.

How does the concept of appointing people to an office (i.e. giving them a label) fit in with the informal, non-hierarchical, relationship-based structure we have just described? Surely if someone is appointed as an elder then he has responsibility for his flock while other elders are responsible for their flocks, and then we end up once again with the same old pyramid structures?

Let there be no doubt about it, the Church of God is desperately in need of Godly leadership. But what is needed is true leaders - gifted and anointed by God - not professional managers who have been trained and appointed by men. From the paucity of any Biblical instructions telling us how to appoint people to the job, we have to conclude that this is not a high priority with God! Instead He seems to be much more concerned with what these wise and experienced people do, rather than what title or position they hold. Let us look at how this works, but please, read this very slowly and carefully as it is very easy to reinterpret this to mean what it does not, simply because of our pre-conceived notions of what leadership is.

When Paul's apostolic team (such as Paul, Barnabas, Silas and those with them) arrived in a new town, such as Antioch of Pisidia Acts 13:14, they preached Christ crucified and lead people into new birth. They then left and moved on to a new town (Acts 13:51). After a while, they then returned to the towns where they had previously preached (Acts 14:21). Finding groups of people who had become steadfast disciples of Jesus Christ, the apostles then appointed, or confirmed the appointment, from among them and some became elders (Acts 14:23). This leads us to two questions: on what basis were some picked and others rejected as elders? Once appointed, what were they to do?

There were two main criteria for choosing the elders. The second of these criteria is the one that is most commonly quoted. It is the moral integrity and purity that is described in 2 Timothy and Titus ("an elder shall be the husband of but one wife....."). Certainly it was important that the elders be people of a steadfast and reliable character that would not use and abuse their position of power, and would not bring the name of Jesus into disrepute. However, this was only the second criterion.

The first prerequisite of being an elder, or leader, of the Church was to have the gifts of leadership. Without the gifts of leadership, however solid and respectable you might be, and however much training you might have, you CANNOT and should not attempt to be a leader! This is very clear from Romans 12:5-8:

> *"so we, being many, are one body in Christ, and individually members of one another. Having then gifts differing according to the grace that is given to us, let us use them: if prophecy, let us prophesy in proportion to our faith; or ministry, let us use it in our ministering; he who teaches, in teaching; he who exhorts, in exhortation; he who gives, with liberality; he who leads, with diligence; he who shows mercy, with cheerfulness."*

It is also clear from Ephesians 4:11-12 that GOD has appointed certain people to be leaders in His Church, to equip and lead people into greater maturity.

> *"And He Himself gave some to be apostles, some prophets, some evangelists, and some pastors and teachers, for the equipping of the saints for the work of ministry, for the edifying of the body of Christ"*

How does God appoint such people? He gives them the gifts. It is impossible to be an anointed evangelist unless you have a gift of evangelism; it is impossible to be an effective teacher unless you have a gift for teaching. This also works the other way around - if God gives you a gift of shepherding (often called pastoring), or prophesy then He also gives you the responsibility to use that gift to His glory and to help others to mature and grow. "To whomsoever much has been given, of him much shall be required" (Luke 12:48 ASV). Of course you can certainly try to be a teacher without the gifting, but those of us who have experienced bad teachers will all know what that is like! You can also try to be a pastor, prophet, apostle or evangelist without the gifting - but in each case you will end up being ineffective and frustrated. Furthermore, your actions will portray a false and un-biblical picture of leadership, which then prevents others from discovering and using the gifts that God has given them.

In appointing some to be elders, Paul and the apostles were not choosing those that they thought would be good for the job, or those who had been trained for the job, they were choosing those who already had been anointed by God for the job. How would they recognize such men? "By your fruits you shall recognize them" (Matt 7:16-20). The evidence of their gifting and their calling was that they were already doing the job - those with the gift of evangelism were already out evangelizing and teaching others to evangelize; those with the gift of shepherding were already out there ministering to the downtrodden and broken-hearted, and teaching others to minister also. In all cases there was the evidence both of the specific gifting and of the gift of leadership that enables them to equip and disciple others in that gift.

This was Jesus' method of discipleship: He would do it (some form of ministry) whilst they observed, He would then allow His disciples to do it while He watched, and then He would send them out to do it by themselves. Every true leader in God's Church should be doing the same. This then is the job of the elders (and indeed, to a lesser extent, of every disciple): to teach others to do the same as the elder is doing. How different that is from what we see the typical "pastor" of a church doing! Note also how personal and time intensive it is. This is not something that leaders can do to a large number of people from a distance - it requires close, individual attention to each disciple, something that cannot be done if you have responsibility for a large "congregation".

We need to be clear, therefore, that these elders were simply appointed as elders among the people that is to say they were NOT given a designated "church" that was their responsibility. Instead they were given as a gift to THE Church, and so, by virtue of the spiritual authority (which comes from a recognition of their gifts, not from a label) they were allowed to have input into any group of believers anywhere. Thus we see Paul giving very direct instructions to the Romans, despite the fact that he had never even met them, and certainly had not been "ordained in their church". To put it in a modern context, what Paul did would be the same as a Baptist missionary in England, without being invited to do so, giving direct instructions to a Pentecostal "church" in America! How many of today's "churches" would permit that?!

We see this also in the difficulty that the Corinthians had with Paul and Apollos. Both were anointed by God. Both were providing leadership to the same group of believers, but the believers had difficulty with the lack of definition and structure and so split themselves into groups - those who followed Paul and those who followed Apollos. Instead, what they were supposed to do was to receive, and combine, the teaching of both apostles. The apostles, and indeed all the other leaders, are in no way in competition with each other, but should serve to complement each other.

Note again that there is no Scriptural support whatsoever for the concept of one pastor in charge of one congregation.

The situation with the deacons is the same. Deacons were people with practical gifts, such as helps, administration, healings, who took up the responsibility of using those gifts to benefit the Church. Since they were already gifted and functioning in their gifting, and since they were also men and women of impeccable character, they were then recognized by being appointed as Deacons. Again, they were a gift to the Church at large, not just to a particular group.

The Internet as an analogy for the Church

Perhaps the best illustration of what the Church is like is the Internet. The Internet is composed of hundreds of thousands of different "nodes" that are interconnected by a communication network. No one controls the internet, yet it operates with a set of common protocols that allow widely different computers (and people) to function in harmony. There is no fixed structure that determines that a certain node may or may not interact with another node however, in practice, one node will most commonly communicate with a handful of others. Because there is no one controlling the internet, it has been able to grow at a phenomenal rate that would never have been possible had there been a central organization.

Of course, the Internet has also provided the opportunity for much that is undesirable and harmful. Indeed, many have suggested that, for this reason, some control structures should be set up. However, such control would be unfeasible, since the Internet is built on relationship rather than hierarchy. And also, any attempts to control it would merely limit the legitimate users, and drive the illegitimate ones underground, where their harmful activities would continue unchecked.

The nodes of the Internet represent the people of the Church. Each one of us can interact with any other believer, but in practice we will tend to associate mostly with a small number that become our friends. The common protocol that we share is the acknowledgement of Jesus as Lord and Saviour. In the true Church there is no central control structure. Instead, out of love and faith, each believer submits to each other, seeking to honor others above themselves, and above all, seeking to please and glorify God.

Imagine for the moment that there were no institutional churches in your town. All the believers would then simply be members of the Church in that town. There would be no need for a name. Fellowship would take place based on people's genuine relationships with each other. Contrast this with the structured relationships that we see in the house church and cell group movement.

Since the members of the Church would meet together on the basis of their relationships, these groupings would be very fluid; at times five meeting here for prayer, at another time three meeting there for Bible study, occasionally 1000 meeting together for celebration. Since their desire is simply to rejoice and grow in God, there would be no reason for people to be jealous of who is meeting with whom, nor how many people they have in any particular group.

All of us have insecurities. We have to be aware that these insecurities prompt us to look for structures and systems to make us feel more secure. This can very quickly lead us back into Babylon. Clearly if we want to remain in, or enter New Jerusalem then we need to find a different way of dealing with these insecurities. Is this not the very healing that Christ offers us as He calls us to rest in Him, casting off our burdens and discovering a self-esteem that is rooted in Him, not in the role which we play? The Kingdom way of dealing with these insecurities is to find a mature believer in whom we trust, who can pray for us, counsel us, and disciple us into our own maturity in Christ.

If we do not do this, then fear is introduced into the equation. Very quickly people start to become jealous, and start to control these fluid relationships. Being fearful that another group is growing bigger or gaining influence, one group may then try to prevent their "members" from going to that group. This is the start of the Babylonian system and, before you know it, they will have given themselves a name, and set themselves up as different (and presumably better) than the other group.

Since the Church will meet on the basis of relationships, there would be no need for any buildings. Meetings will take place wherever seems to be most suitable. Most of the time this would be in people's homes. At times it might be necessary to rent a public building. Without the ongoing expenses of buildings, or of professional leaders, the people's financial generosity can go directly into ministering to the poor or reaching the unreached.

God is a God of infinite diversity. He has created billions of people, each one of us different, and placed us in thousands of different cultures. Diversity and difference is not wrong, so we must learn not to feel threatened by other people's differences. Instead we can view them as opportunities for us to learn. Without diversity to challenge us, our perspectives would be very limited!

Among the people of this Church of no name, God will anoint some as leaders, those in whom He has deposited the gift. Some will be gifted as evangelists, others shepherds, prophets, teachers, apostles. How would we know who they are? They will not draw attention to themselves. They will not set themselves up and tell people that they must submit to them. But they will be known by their fruits; those that are building the believers up into maturity (Eph 4) are, *de facto*, the leaders. These leaders will also relate informally to each other, submitting one to another, not jostling for position or trying to outrank each other.

It is important to note that the only difference between a "leader" and a "follower" is the gifting that the Lord has deposited within him or her. Since there is no extra status to being a leader, nor any financial advantage, and since there is no organization to run, those that are not leaders would have no motivation for trying to pretend that they are. How different from the Babylonian "church" structures we see around us! This is the Kingdom of God in action, The New Jerusalem.

On your second reading we would suggest that you stop at this point and spend some time praying and meditating about the things you have read and how they apply to you. The following questions may help you in this process:

1) See how many Scripture references you can find in the New Testament that validates the concept of church membership.
2) At what period in history did things start to go wrong and why?
3) If ministry is based on the natural overflow of gifts and anointings that the Lord has placed in us, explain the modern day role of the professional Pastor in the light of the New Testament.
4) Why does the Babylonian church place such an important emphasis on who is permitted to serve communion, and baptize new believers?

Chapter 10

NUMERICAL GROWTH

Things that are alive grow. The body of Christ is a living organism and it too will grow in size. This will not occur because of artificial programs in which we force people to listen to our doctrines and teachings about God. It will occur quite naturally as we share our lives with others. Doctrine teaches people about Christ, but in order to be born again, people need to meet with Christ. They will do that as they get to know us, and how we live, for Christ lives in us and shines through us. Certainly doctrine is important, but it has been demonstrated time and time again, that the most effective form of evangelism is that of one individual sharing his life and his joy with another individual.

We see this in Acts. When the Church was scattered throughout the region by persecution, each disciple took the gospel with him, and so we see in Acts 19 that when Paul arrived in Ephesus the gospel had already arrived there before him. How? By the natural spread of disciples "gossiping the Gospel" wherever they went. Certainly some are called to be preachers like Paul, but every believer is called to be a witness - someone who tells what he has seen, heard, and experienced.

However, there is a big trap here. It is "God that gives the increase" not us! Yet almost every church on Earth has numerical growth as one of its goals. To focus on the growth takes us away from the focus that Jesus gave us. In the Great Commission we are instructed to "go... and make disciples". But we cannot make hundreds of disciples, as the process of discipleship involves intimate relationships, and we cannot do that with more than a handful of believers. As we will see, it is this desire to try to have a small number of professionals teaching a large number of laymen that has been one of the major factors in the development of our false concepts of church.

On your second reading we would suggest that you stop at this point and spend some time praying and meditating about the things you have read and how they apply to you. The following questions may help you in this process:

1) When you think of evangelism, do you think in terms of getting people saved and into regular "church fellowship", or of seeing them grow into mature committed believers?
2) Does having a large congregation indicate that God is blessing a church?
3) If you lead someone to accepting Jesus as his Saviour and Lord, which outcome would you prefer to see?

a) He attends church regularly, has joined the midweek Bible study, and is a member of the church choir. Every day he starts the morning with 10 minutes reading a devotional booklet. He no longer has any friends that are not church goers, and avoids any situations that might bring him into contact with non-believers, *(for example, bars, discos, sports clubs)*, or,
b) He does not organized meetings. However, he studies the Bible in depth every day and spends an hour a day

in prayer - either by himself or with a handful of good friends with whom he shares his struggles and his joys. When not at home with his family and friends, he will usually be found mixing with unbelievers - he has joined a darts club, and enjoys spending time (perhaps in a bar) with his work colleagues after work. Many times if they are going through difficulties, for example a divorce, it will be this disciple that they will call upon for help and support, and often, as a result, they will themselves enter the Kingdom of God. *Which was Jesus' way? Which is our way?*

Chapter 11

ESCAPING THROUGH THE FIRE

"By the grace God has given me, I laid a foundation as an expert builder, and someone else is building on it. But each one should be careful how he builds. For no one can lay any other foundation other than the one already laid, which is Jesus Christ. If any man builds on this foundation using gold, silver, costly stones, wood, hay, or straw, his work will be shown for what it is, because the Day will bring it to light. It will be revealed with fire, and the fire will test the quality of each man's work. If what he has built survives, he will receive his reward. If it is burned up, he will suffer loss; he himself will be saved, but only as one escaping through the flames." (1 Cor 3:10-15).

Praise God, we serve a mighty risen King whose patience, compassion, and love is not only poured out freely for us, but is without end! Within the Babylonian church system there are many millions of Godfearing, born-again, spirit-filled, true believers: pastors, seminary teachers, Sunday school superintendents, church wardens, deacons, ushers,... the list is endless. Each one of these is loved by God and is precious in His sight. None is favoured over any other. We give thanks to God for His grace and mercy which He showers on us, an undeserving people. The Bible teaches us that ALL have fallen short of the glory of God, yet He embraces us, uses us, and has a vision for us. Many of us continue in the daily struggle to overcome sin, to resist the devil, to cast down evil imaginations. Yet we know that in all these trials we are more than conquerors.

How fortunate we are that God does not wait until we are perfect (although we are in Him). The process of sanctification is the school of discipleship that lasts a lifetime. At whatever point along this journey we might be, God has His plans and uses us to bring about His purposes on Earth. If the above is true, and we know it to be so, why then should we be so concerned that the church is imperfect? Knowing that God continues to work with and use us while we are still imperfect, why should the same not also be true of the church?

There is, however, a fundamental difference between the two. We, as believers, are "born-again". We are no longer the old carnal people that we used to be. *"If anyone is in Christ he is a new creation; the old has gone, the new has come!"* (2 Cor 5:17) "Our old self was crucified with him so that the body of sin might be rendered powerless" (Rom 6.6). Although we still struggle with the shadows of the old sinful self, from God's perspective we have been created in righteousness (Eph 4:24). The seed of the resurrection body has been placed in us, and our eternal future is life, not death. Since our future is to be with God, He does not wait until we arrive in heaven before He starts to work with us and through us. NO! He starts from the moment that we are born again!

Not so with the structures of Babylon! Everything that is of this Earth will be swept away! (see Heb 1:10-12; Rev 21:1). These are temporary structures that have no validity in the New Earth. God is preparing us for His heavenly Kingdom, and His perfect plan is that we should be experiencing that Kingdom life here on Earth. Christ has given His life to us (His body, His Church) to "present her to Himself as a radiant Church, without stain or wrinkle or any other blemish, but holy and blameless." (Eph 5:27).

As we have seen, the Babylonian structures are not what God had in mind! He has no interest in preserving them. Furthermore, they are actually a major hindrance to people maturing and growing as Christians, and they also prevent unbelievers from seeing the true Kingdom in action, or being part of it. Having said that, we also need to understand that God uses us as we are. He does not wait until we are perfect, and indeed He leads us through experiences in order to give us the opportunities to learn from them and to grow in maturity.

To understand this, we need to distinguish between the perfect and the permissive will of God. For example, it was not God's perfect will that David committed adultery with Bathsheba. But He did permit it to happen. Why? Because when David repented, he learned from the experience, and subsequently was called a man after God's heart. As it is with us, it is not God's perfect will that we sin, but we do - each one of us struggles with temptations: the lusts of the flesh, the pride of life. God permits us to fail, and through these failures, if we are seeking after Him, we learn. But this is not God's perfect will. His perfect will is that we live by faith; overcoming the enemy at every juncture, living fully in tune with His spirit. In the entire history of man, it is only Jesus who has attained this perfect standard. So, in God's permissive will, He allows the Babylonian structures to continue.

Revelation is Progressive

When we are born again into God's Kingdom, we do not arrive in full maturity. On the contrary; we start as babies who need spoon feeding. With time, however, it is expected that we should grow up (see Heb 5:12-14). This happens as, little by little, we gain more revelation and more understanding of who God is, who we are, and what God has done and is doing. Even so, however long we are on this Earth, our understanding is always partial. As we read the Scriptures and as we hear from God, our interpretation of what He says is always filtered through the perspectives of our personality and our cultural heritage. This makes it very difficult, if not almost impossible, to hear the pure Word of God, for *"now we see in a mirror, dimly, but then face to face"* (1 Cor 13,12).

If our whole upbringing has conditioned us to associate Christianity with the "churches" we see around us, it will be difficult for us to jump straight into a revelation of the things we have been discussing in this book. Indeed, such understanding will only come through a painful process of sorting out what is of God and what is of the World. Yet even as we go through that process, God still loves us, and still delights in blessing us.

For example, being a new believer who is earnestly seeking after God, you might join yourself to a babylonian church, honestly believing it to be God's will for you. Given your limited understanding at that time, the only other option that you could consider would be to have no fellowship of any sort. Knowing this, God allows you to join the "church" and may even bless you mightily in it, perhaps also using you to be a tremendous blessing to others also. Does this mean that it is God's perfect will for you to be in that "church"? No, but He permits it, and even extends His mercy so that, "in all things God works for the good of those who love Him" (Rom 8:28).

Should it so happen that, at the same time, there are many other members of that same "church" that God is also blessing, then the church might go through a period of rapid growth and apparent "success". Does this mean that God is approving of and blessing this so-called "church"? Or does it merely mean that at this time and place He is prepared to use it, or more importantly the people in it, to further His purposes. We see this principle at work in both the Old and New Testaments.

In the Old, we see God raising up ungodly conquerors to be his instruments of discipleship and chastisement for Israel (see, for example, how God uses Assyria as an instrument of His judgment against Israel, but then brings judgment against Assyria for their pride and rebellion - Is 10:5-12).

In the New, we see that Jesus and Paul are quite happy to let people preach the Gospel despite their impure motives, since God can still use them to get His message out (Mark 9:38-41 & Php 1:15-18).

We must be very careful, therefore, that we do not jump to false conclusions. Just because a particular ministry or "church" is having tremendous results for the Kingdom and seems to be receiving a real blessing from God, we cannot jump to the conclusion that therefore God is happy with the institution.

What, then, of the countless, genuine believers who have sought God's guidance and have felt led to enter "full-time ministry". Often they will have had their call confirmed by other mature believers. Were they wrong? Did they not receive a genuine call from God? Or, given the limitations of their understanding and revelation at that time, did this represent God's best option for them?

We are in no position to judge the motives and decisions of others. We can only look to ourselves, and then we have to be thankful to God for His tremendous patience with us, as we have failed time and time again to enter into His *"good, pleasing, and perfect will"* (Rom 12:2).

So where does this leave us? whether in Babylon or out, God loves us. He will continue to love us. Ultimately He will draw all His true believers to Himself in the Heavenly Kingdom. If we have built a foundation on Jesus, we will be saved. But let each one of us look to see how we are building on that foundation. Are we building Babylonian structures of wood and hay that will be burnt away? Or are we building Kingdom relationships of pure gold that we will carry with us into the New Jerusalem?

Chapter 12

THE END - AND THE BEGINNING

There is much more that could have been included in this book - discussions about true discipleship, the restoration of those that have sinned, the qualities of true leadership. However, instead of discussing these in detail, I have attempted to raise some issues and provoke some thought that will lead you to seek and find more answers for yourself.

Across the globe there are countless thousands of Christians who have been asking the same questions as you. At the heart of every sincere and truth-seeking believer there is a desire for more of God. The Bible teaches us that those who are seeking, and continue to seek, will find. If your seeking has led you to ask some of the questions that I have discussed in this book, then it is important to understand that it is God Himself who is leading you on this journey. It is the Holy Spirit that leads people out of Babylon and into the New Jerusalem. For Chris and I, this journey has been a difficult and tortuous route, but around every corner and over every brow we have seen the Holy Spirit encouraging us and confirming to us that we are headed in the right direction.

At times it has been difficult to find others to talk to, people who would understand. Often we have asked ourselves if indeed our critics have been right, that it is us who have gone astray and failed to conform to God's will. On each occasion, we have been led back into the Scriptures where we have seen yet again Jesus confronting the religious systems that victimized, abused, and bound people that He Himself had come to set free.

As the Lord has led us to others who are on the same journey, it has been no surprise to us to hear them describing very similar struggles. Some, after much soul searching, have chosen to leave the established structures of Babylon. Others we have met, who had started on the same journey, have turned back, preferring the security of Babylon to the rejection and accusations that seem to be an integral part of this journey. A few, on raising questions that have been perceived as a threat to the status quo, have been forcibly ejected and excommunicated from their "churches".

It has been our discovery that those who successfully find their way out of Babylon and into the New Jerusalem have been those who are "seekers". Their overriding motivation has been to seek truth and reality, at whatever cost. Unfortunately, many who have started on this journey have been so hurt and wounded by the rejections and accusations they have faced that they have fallen by the wayside, discouraged, bitter, and ultimately backslidden.

For most of us the process of coming out of Babylon is slow and painful. The longer we have spent in the organized, structured church system, the harder it is for us to come to terms with the revelation that so much of it is not only unbiblical but is actually harmful both to those caught up in it, who are held captive and prevented from entering the true freedoms of Christ, and also to the unbelievers outside who get a false picture of the teachings of Christ, and are therefore inoculated against the true Gospel of the Kingdom.

Since revelation is progressive, and since it comes only by the mercy and grace of God, we must be patient and not critical of our friends and neighbors who do not yet see and understand what we have come to believe as true. Often this may produce great loneliness for us, as we cannot share with those we love, the things that are so fresh and full of life for us. You may find that you need to voluntarily withdraw yourself from the company of fellow believers, or you may find yourself involuntarily thrown out of fellowship by people who you once regarded as friends. In either case, do not be discouraged. You are not alone, thousands of other believers are on the same journey. Draw your strength from the Lord, and persist in seeking after truth.

Be wise and discerning about whom you take into your confidence. Often, as people ask you why you are doing this or not doing that, it may be better not to try to explain. You will often be misunderstood. At these times you will be needing to pray along with Francis of Assisi. "O Divine Master, grant that I may not so much seek to be consoled as to console; to be understood as to understand; to be loved as to love."

Be strong in the Lord, knowing that it is He who will empower and enable you. Be courageous. Do not give up. In time the Lord will lead you to others who are going through the same process and you will enter into the sunshine of the New Jerusalem.

WEBSITE LINKS:

www.enlightened.org.uk/religious.html
www.therealchurch.com/index.html
www.truthortradition.com
www.freechristianbook.ca
www.angelfire.com/fl3/gammadim/wpasynagogueofsatan.
   html *(Prophetic radio station)*

REFERENCE BOOKS:

Pagan Christianity Frank Viola (Dyndale Publishing)
Apostles & Prophets, Dr. Bill Hamon, 1997 Destiny Image Publishers
W. E. Vines Expository Dictionary of New Testament words
The Early Church, Henry Chadwick, 1967, Penguin Books, London
The Open Church, James H. Rutz, 1992, Seed Sowers, Beaumont, TX USA.
Beyond Radical, Gene Edwards Seed Sowers, 2006 Beaumont, TX USA
Documents of the Christian Church, Ed. Henry Bettenson, 1963, Oxford University Press.
A History of the Christian Church, Williston Walker et al. 1985, Charles Scribner's Sons, New York

Printed in the United States
137927LV00001B/6/P